Choices for the carer of an elderly relative

Carers Handbook Series

Choices for the carer of an elderly relative

Marina Lewycka

BOOKS

© 1995 Marina Lewycka
Published by Age Concern England
1268 London Road
London SW16 4ER

First published 1995 in Age Concern Books' *Caring in a Crisis* series
This edition published 1998

Editor Caroline Hartnell
Production Vinnette Marshall
Designed and typeset by GreenGate Publishing Services, Tonbridge, Kent
Printed in Great Britain by Bell & Bain Ltd, Glasgow

A catalogue record for this book is available from the British Library.

ISBN 0-86242-263-9

Bulk orders

Age Concern England is pleased to offer customised editions of all its titles to UK
companies, institutions or other organisations wishing to make a bulk purchase.
For further information, please contact the Publishing Department at the address
above. Tel: 0181-679 8000. Fax: 0181-679 6069. E-mail: addisom@ace.org.uk

Contents

About the author

Marina Lewycka is a lecturer and freelance writer. She contributed to the BBC handbook *Who Cares Now?* and her training resource pack *Survival Skills for Carers* is published by the National Extension College with support from the Department of Health. She has been involved in the organisation of weekend courses for carers. She is also the author of two other books in the Carers Handbook Series: *The Carer's Handbook: What to do and who to turn to* and *Finding and paying for residential and nursing home care*.

Acknowledgements

This book could not have happened without the help of the many people who have contributed their ideas, insights and experiences. In particular I would like to thank David Moncrieff, Sarah Butler, Evelyn McEwen and Caroline Hartnell for their help in shaping the original idea, and Caroline and Evelyn for their continuing support in seeing the idea through all its difficult stages. I would like to thank Francine Bates of the Carers National Association and Dorothy Berry-Lound of the HOST Consultancy for their helpful comments on the text; Jane Whelan, Lorna Easterbrook, Audrey King and Rashida Bharmal of Age Concern England for their expert comments; and Vinnette Marshall for sympathetic and helpful work on the copy.

I am very grateful for the help that I received from the many people here in Sheffield in the health service, the local authority housing and social services departments and voluntary organisations, especially Dr Kate Richards, Brenda Earl from the Carers' Centre, Sue Moss and Janet Graham from the Sheffield Carers' Support Group, Beth Cole from the Alzheimer's Disease Society and Pam Walton from New Ways to Work.

Above all I would like to thank the carers who spoke to me so openly about their own situations. The book is a tribute to their willingness not only to help their own relatives but, by sharing their experiences with others, to help guide other carers through the difficult maze of choices which they have had to make. I have withheld their names for reasons of confidentiality, but you know who you are – and thank you!

Introduction

As our parents get older, many of us will be faced with difficult choices about how best to care for them. Being a carer can mean so many different things – from living at a distance and keeping a check on things to taking on a full-time caring role. We may find ourselves having to balance conflicting needs, priorities and expectations within the family. While the range of options is greater than ever, choosing between them has also become much more complex.

Since the war, society has been changing in a number of ways which affect how we care for older people. Families nowadays are much smaller, with fewer people of working age to share the care of the older generation; more women, the traditional carers, go out to work. Families are more mobile: more people move away from their home town in search of work, leaving their parents behind. There are more family breakdowns, with almost one in three marriages ending in divorce. People's expectations have also changed. Privacy, space and leisure time to oneself are taken for granted. All these changes have made families more fragmented or 'nuclear', and this affects our decisions about the way older people are cared for.

Another major change is that with better health care more people are living longer into old age. There are more older people needing care at the same time as there are fewer younger people around to look after them. The welfare state can no longer bridge all the gaps. Instead, when a crisis strikes, it is often left to each family to cope as best it can. The strain may fall on just one or two people – the carers.

It is estimated that about 6 million people in Britain are carers, and that one in five people aged between 45 and 64 are caring for someone, usually an elderly relative. Arrangements for caring for an older person are often made under pressure, without time to consider all the options. It is not surprising, therefore, that many arrangements break down, or lead to great stress and sometimes bitterness.

This book is written for people whose parents or other relatives are getting older or have become ill, and who are wondering what is the best way of caring for them. It encourages you to look at your own circumstances, priorities and personality and to choose the caring role which seems best suited to you as well as to your relative. It does not recommend one 'ideal' solution, but looks at the whole range of care options, including family care, social services, health services and private and voluntary sector provision, and shows how they all interlink.

The person you care for will be referred to as 'she' throughout this book, but everything that is said applies equally to both sexes.

1 Deciding about caring

Some people become carers suddenly when their relative develops an illness or has an accident. Others make a more considered choice to look after an older relative. For many people, becoming a carer is not a decision they consciously make – it just happens gradually as someone close to them becomes more ill or dependent.

Being a carer may mean caring for someone most of the time, or it may mean arranging care which will be provided by others. The family, the local authority, the National Health Service, voluntary bodies, private agencies, residential and nursing homes – all have a part to play. Whether you decide to become a carer, or whether it is something you have grown into, you still have choices about how much and what kind of care you will give.

This chapter looks at what is involved in caring and helps you to assess yourself and your situation, so that you can make a clearer choice between the options open to you and your relative.

Harry

'I was in a terrible dilemma. I wanted to do the right thing for my family and the right thing for Mum. But there was another worry lurking at the back of my mind.'

After his father died, Harry's mother lived alone in the house for several years. She seemed to be managing all right. She had her network of friends, and she was always going out somewhere. Until one day she slipped and fell down stairs and broke her hip. She was on the floor in terrible pain and had to drag herself to the telephone to call the ambulance.

'That experience really shook her. When I went in to hospital to see her I almost didn't recognise her. She looked awful – all shrunk and aged, not like my strong independent-minded Mum at all. I didn't know what to do. It seemed impossible to let her go back to living on her own, but I knew she wouldn't accept the idea of going into a home. There seemed to be only one other option. As we came away from the hospital, my wife said, 'You know, if you want her to come and live with us, that's all right by me.' But there was something about the way she said it. She's never got on too well with my Mum – she finds her very dominating. Our younger son was still living at home, studying for his A levels, and his friends were always round the house. When I asked him how he would feel about having his gran to live there, he didn't say anything, but his face said it all. He went very quiet. Then after a long while he said, 'What room would she have?' Of course the one person I didn't consult was Mum. I felt I couldn't, in case she said she really wanted to come and live with us.

'I was in a terrible dilemma. I wanted to do the right thing for my family and the right thing for Mum. But there was another worry lurking at the back of my mind. When I was a teenager, I went a bit wild, and we had quite a stormy relationship. I wasn't sure what it would be like living with her again after all these years.

'In the end I went to see our GP, and he put me on to the social worker at the hospital, who was very helpful. She said there was a whole range of options for my Mum, apart from going into a home or living with me. Her suggestion was that Mum could carry on living at home and have carers coming in. This seemed like an ideal solution. However, when the occupational therapist visited the house, she said the stairs were very steep, and suggested Mum might be better off in a bungalow. Luckily, a place in a sheltered bungalow near to her home came up. Mum grumbled a bit, but the bungalow was so nice I think she realised she was lucky. Also, she may have had her doubts about coming to live with us or going back to live in her old house. The bungalow is very new, purpose-built round a little courtyard, and wired up to an alarm system with a pull-cord in every room, and a warden calls in regularly. She can still keep up with her friends and her activities – she even has a small garden of her own to look after. But no stairs.

'When she first came out of hospital the district nurse called every day, and she had someone from social services to help her get out of bed in the mornings and back to bed at night. I took some time off work to help her move in and get settled. But now she's on her feet again she just has a home help once a week, which we pay for, and for the time being she's managing fine. My wife or I visit at the weekend, and of course we're always there on the end of a phone if she needs us. As the time comes when she needs more care, she can have carers coming to her at home. And after that ... well, we'll see.'

What is a carer?

There are many different ways of caring for someone. You may decide it is better to live away from the person you care for, or you may choose to live with them, or you may already be living together as part of a family. The job of looking after older relatives may be taken on by one or more family members, or by people outside the family. Being a carer may mean:

- living at a distance, organising care for your relative in her own home, and keeping a check on things by telephone. This might involve setting up a network of carers, which could include family members, social services staff and paid helpers;
- living nearby and looking in regularly;
- living with the person you care for;
- arranging care for your relative in a residential or nursing home, and visiting regularly to keep an eye on things.

Carers – whether family members or people outside the family – may take on many different roles. These include:

- communicating with other people who look after your relative;
- handling money matters: collecting a pension, paying bills, etc;

- filling in forms and handling paperwork related to housing, legal matters and benefits;
- helping with domestic chores such as shopping, cooking, laundry and cleaning;
- making sure your relative takes prescribed medication regularly;
- helping with personal care, such as getting washed and dressed, bathing, hair care and foot care, brushing teeth, using the toilet.

Many carers take on a combination of these roles and responsibilities, and these may change over time. It is important to think carefully about yourself as a carer, and about how caring fits in with the rest of your life. The self-assessment section on pages 5–17 may help you work out which caring pattern is best for you and your relative.

What's it like being a carer?

Whichever way of caring you choose, there are no easy options. Living with the person you care for may result in extreme stress and physical exhaustion.

Mary

'The doctor prescribed some tranquillisers for him. I know this is wrong, but when I get desperate I take them myself.'

Living at a distance may mean constant worry and feelings of guilt that you are not doing enough.

Dawn

'We thought of having her to live with us, but it wasn't really practical because of the stairs. I went to see her every day. We had three phones put in, so wherever I was in the house I would hear if she rang. But I still couldn't relax. I was always worried about her.'

All carers have their own experiences of caring, and their own ways of surviving.

Alison

'It's the small things that help you keep going. Last time, when she was in hospital, amid all the crisis, one nurse said to me, 'Hasn't she got lovely skin?' I could have hugged her. A few kind words make all the difference. It's so important to see something positive, amid all the negativity. Sometimes you have to laugh else you'd cry. Sometimes you do cry.'

Yourself as a carer: How much should you take on?

Before you make any decisions about caring for your relative it's a good idea to spend a bit of time looking at yourself – your own priorities, your personal and family circumstances, your health, your personality and that of your relative, and, crucially, how you get on with your relative. Even if you are already caring for someone, you may decide that a different way of caring would be better. Remember, your caring role may last for a few weeks or months, or you may find yourself caring for your relative for years.

Assessing yourself as a carer

The questions below are designed to focus your thoughts and help you decide how much care and what kind of care you are best able to give. It is a good idea to talk through the choices facing you with someone who is not involved in the decision – a good friend, or your doctor, or a social worker or counsellor. You could start by discussing your answers to these questions.

1 What are my priorities?

Sometimes we get so caught up in immediate problems that it's hard to step back and reflect on which direction we really want to go in. These questions are designed to get you thinking about what is really important in your life. Try numbering them 1–8 (or more if there are other things you would like to do) or just spend some time thinking about them.

Order of priority

I want to spend time with my partner and/or children.

I want to look after my relative.

I want to get ahead in my career.

I want to undertake a course of study/work training.

I want to travel.

I want to develop a sport/leisure/musical/artistic/ creative interest.

I want to get my home sorted out the way I would like it to be.

Other

Food for thought

You will probably want to do several of these things, but putting them in order of priority can help you work out what is really important to you, even though you know that compromises may have to be made and that things do not always work out the way you would like. It's all too easy as a carer to put others first all the time. Never forget that your own life, and your own desires and ambitions, are just as important as those of your relative and the other people in your family.

Joan

'We visit regularly, we organise her shopping, and we get someone to come in and do the garden. But my sister and I both have full-time jobs. When mother got ill the hospital just assumed we would be able to drop everything in order to look after her. I'm sure they wouldn't have assumed that if we were men.'

Dawn

'I was keeping Mum happy, keeping my husband happy, keeping my children happy. Sometimes I wondered, 'Where do I fit in?' But I knew it wasn't going to last for ever. I kept my job on, even though at times it was very hard. I've taken a course in aromatherapy – I'm preparing for the next thing.'

2 How well do I get on with my relative?

However well you get on with someone, living with them is bound to put extra strains on your relationship. These questions are to help you decide whether your relationship would survive the strain.

What is the longest unbroken stretch of time you have spent with your relative?

How did you get on at the beginning, and how did you get on at the end?

Which of these statements applies to your relationship with your relative (tick those which apply):

- She's like my best friend.
- Despite all the pain and difficulty, we still enjoy each other's company.
- I love her dearly but she drives me crazy.
- We get on well at first, but after a short while we start arguing.
- We get on fine so long as we can get away from each other from time to time.
- We get on fine so long as we don't see too much of each other.
- I find some of her habits very irritating.
- We've never really got on, and her illness has brought out the tension between us.
- I've never forgiven her for things that happened in the past.

Food for thought

All of us have times when we feel intense irritation with someone we live with. This is particularly true if we cannot express our irritation so we let it build up. At the same time, older people may feel frustrated at losing their independence and power, when they see younger people taking on the roles which were once theirs. Parents may resent being upstaged by their children. This may make them more demanding. It is often the only way they have of asserting themselves. People suffering from Alzheimer's disease have particular problems, and may undergo personality changes, so even if you got on well with your relative before, you may find it increasingly difficult to feel loving towards her as her illness progresses.

For all these reasons, it is important to be realistic about how much time you would like to spend with your relative. Everybody is different in this respect. Much will depend on your personality (check your answers to question 1) and the nature of your relative's illness or disability. If you think it is likely that you will often feel irritated, and that you will let your irritation show, it may be better for everyone if you set up a caring routine which minimises this, for example caring at a distance or residential care.

Zahira

'She laughs when she gets things wrong. She's got two teeth missing at the front and she's got such a cheeky smile. We all tease her. She likes a joke.'

Joan

'I didn't have a happy childhood, and in many ways I blame my mother for that. Even though it's all in the past, I still feel quite angry towards her, and I suppose that comes out when we're together for any length of time.'

3 How much time do I have?

Before making any decisions about caring, you need to make a realistic estimate of how much spare time you have. The first step is to try to work out how long you spend on various activities.

There are 168 hours in a week, so if you subtract your total from 168 you will have an idea of how many spare hours you have. It is also useful to look at when your spare time is – during the day, in the evenings, or at weekends. This will help you to choose a pattern of caring that will fit in with the rest of your life.

Time spent per week: *Hours*

sleeping
_____

working (including travel)
_____

preparing and eating meals
_____

chores/housework
_____

shopping
_____

childcare
_____

family activities
_____

relaxation and leisure
_____

pottering about
_____

other
_____

                          Total
_____

Food for thought

If you try to squeeze more commitments into an already busy life, something else inevitably has to give way. It may seem easiest to cut out those times when we don't seem to be doing anything very much – the times we have for relaxing and unwinding. But this may be a 'false economy' of time, if we just end up feeling very stressed. All of us need time just to potter around and recharge our batteries.

If you have no spare hours, or very few, you may be able to think of chores you could cut down on. Or you may have to think of getting more help from other people, rather than taking on too much day-to-day caring yourself. Working and caring can be particularly tiring, so be sure to leave yourself time to rest.

Alison

'If I had time off work I always made the hours up another time. But it was very tiring.'

Gill

'I'm quite well organised, but it's sometimes a strain. I'm going to give up my job – then I'll have more time to look after her.'

4 What is my own health like?

If you are considering being a carer, it's important to make sure that you have the strength and stamina. Caring is often both emotionally draining and physically exhausting, and carers sometimes develop back problems from lifting someone heavy. The following are some of the questions you should consider.

	Yes	No
Am I currently being treated for any serious medical condition?		
If so, could it affect my ability to care?		
Have I received treatment for a serious medical condition within the last five years?		
If so, could it recur?		
Have I ever received treatment for an emotional or psychological condition, for example nerves, anxiety, depression, insomnia?		
Do I get tired easily?		
Do I often get out of breath when I walk?		
Would I have difficulty lifting my relative?		

Food for thought

If your answer is 'Yes' to any of these questions, it is important for you to talk to your GP before you take on any caring commitments. If you are already a carer, make sure that your GP knows about the pressures you are under. If you will need to lift or turn your relative, make sure you get advice from a district nurse or physiotherapist about the best way of doing this to avoid back injury.

> ### Gill
>
> 'It was a difficult time for me – I think it is for a lot of women – going through the menopause, coping with their children growing up and leaving home, and suddenly there's this new set of demands.'

> ### Ellen
>
> 'I've been ill myself. The doctor says I suffer from stress, and I have a lot of trouble with my knees; I can't get around as well as I used to. I have to take tablets. The first time he went into respite care, that was the first time I went to the doctor for something to do with me.'

5 What skills and resources do I have?

This section looks at some of the factors which could make your life as a carer easier. Don't worry if you haven't got all the skills or resources listed below. Once you start caring for someone you will soon develop skills you never knew you had.

	Yes	No	Occasionally
Car (or access to car and driver)			
Telephone			
Enough money to be able to afford extra help if necessary			

Helpful spouse/children

Helpful brothers and sisters

Helpful neighbours

Experience of working with older people

Skill at running a household

Skill at managing money

Skill at writing letters and doing paperwork

Skill at getting people to do things

Organisational and time management skills

Knowledge of how the system works

Knowledge of nursing

Other

Food for thought

If you know you have particular strong points, it is a good idea to set up a pattern of caring that builds on them. There may also be other members of your family who have talents and resources, and would be willing to make them available. See pages 33–34 for ideas about involving the rest of the family.

Alison

'I see coping with Mum as a problem-solving exercise. Often there are quite simple practical solutions to problems. For example to stop her wandering we put a heavy spring on the garden gate.'

6 What is my financial position?

Caring for someone may involve you in a lot of extra expenses, some of which you may not have thought of. See pages 43–54 for a breakdown of some of the costs you may face.

Which of the following statements apply to you?

	Yes	No
I can afford to give up my job.		
I have a lot of other financial commitments at the moment.		
I could do with the extra money from the Invalid Care Allowance (see pp 79–80).		
I am comfortably off and could manage the extra expense of caring.		
I would really struggle to meet the extra expense involved.		
My relative is comfortably off, and could meet some of the expenses from her income.		
I would feel awkward or embarrassed asking my relative to pay for things.		

Food for thought

If you are going to be struggling financially, it is important that you set up a pattern of caring that does not leave you much worse off. For example, if you are going out to work and you need the money you earn, then do not commit yourself to a pattern of caring that would result in you having to give up your job. On the other hand, if you are under 65 and not working, and you are prepared to care for your relative for 35 hours or more a week, then you may find the extra income from the Invalid Care Allowance useful. See pages 62–65 for information about combining caring and working.

Betty

'With us both being at home all day, we were running up a fortune in heating bills.'

> ### Alison
>
> 'Fortunately I was able to take early retirement. If I hadn't then I think Mum would have had to go into a home. We're not well off, but we have enough to manage.'

7 How good would I be at day-to-day caring?

Caring for someone on a day-to-day basis is as much a matter of personality as a matter of commitment. Some people take to it naturally; other people, however good their intentions, find that they are just not cut out for a caring role. Most people fall somewhere between these two extremes. These questions are designed to help you decide whether you have the right temperament to be a carer.

	Yes	*No*
I am very patient. I can't remember when I last lost my temper.		
I am usually cheerful. It takes a lot to upset me.		
I am good at juggling several tasks.		
If I get irritated I never let my irritation show.		
I am not squeamish – I could cope with personal or intimate tasks such as toileting or handling soiled laundry.		
I can cope with stress and keep cool under pressure.		

Food for thought

Only a saint would answer 'Yes' to all these questions. But if any of your answers are 'No' you need to think in advance of ways of avoiding situations which are going to bring out the worst in you. In particular, you should think twice about living with someone if there is going to be constant friction between you.

Norah

'Sometimes when I prepare a meal for her, she just eats a little, then she leaves it. My sister can't cope with that. She says, 'You let mother bully you.' She's very different by nature, and she gets angry more quickly. But it doesn't bother me. I have a lot of patience. I worked with old people at a lunch club before and I loved it.'

Anne

'I have to take her to the toilet. Sometimes she doesn't remember to wipe her bottom, so now we do it together. She does the front and I do the back. My sister can't do it – she's more squeamish than me.'

8 How about living with my relative?

Practical questions such as how much room you have in your home are just one factor in deciding how and where you care for your relative. Just as important are your feelings about living with your relative, so bear in mind your answers to question 2, about how well you get on with your relative, when completing this section.

	Yes	*No*
Is there a spare room in my house that my relative could live in?		
Would I need to make alterations to the house if my relative were to move in?		
Would I be prepared to move into my relative's house?		
Would I be prepared to move to a different house so that my relative could live with us?		
Would I be prepared to move to a different house so that my relative could live in a flat or annexe attached to the house?		

Food for thought

Even if it would be practically possible, you may still decide that you really don't want to live with your relative. There is more about the different housing options on pages 34–41, and information about making alterations to your home on pages 48–50.

Alison

'I couldn't cope if she lived here, and I don't think she'd want to. Her own home is more suitable, and safer. She couldn't manage the stairs to the bathroom here.'

---

9 How would my taking on a day-to-day caring role affect my partner and children?

Whichever way you care for your relative, there are bound to be extra pressures on your partner and children. Ask yourself how much you will expect them to help. Even if it's just sitting with your relative while you go out, or preparing their own meals once in a while, or taking on chores which you would normally do, their lives will inevitably be affected, so it is important to consult them. Which of the following statements apply to your family?

	Yes	*No*
My partner/children are fond of their relative, and like to have her around.		
My partner/children find their relative's eccentric behaviour difficult to cope with.		
My partner/children will give me plenty of support in my caring role.		
My partner/children will feel embarrassed about bringing their friends home if their relative is there.		
My partner/children will feel resentful if I am able to give them less attention.		

My partner/children find her very irritating.

I would expect my partner/children to look
after themselves more.

I would expect my partner/children to help
look after their relative.

Food for thought

Families can be very different in the way they respond to older relatives. Children, in particular, may find an eccentric grandparent lovable and amusing, or they may find her frightening and embarrassing. Your partner's feelings will be coloured by his or her own relationship with your relative, and also his or her own work pressures and expectations of support from you. But bear in mind that they may say what they think they ought to say, or what you expect them to say, rather than what they really feel.

10 What would be my reasons for caring for my relative myself?

Norah

'My husband has been very supportive, but I'm careful to make time for him as well as my mother. I'm aware that when he retires and he's at home all day, which won't be long now, things will be different.'

Some people, especially daughters and daughters-in-law, may come under great pressure from their families, or from doctors or social workers, to become full-time carers. Others feel bound by promises made to a dying parent to look after their surviving partner. Yet others feel it's the right and natural thing for them to do. You may feel that a number of these statements apply to you, but try to put them in order of priority to give you a clearer idea whether caring for your relative is something you would choose, or something you feel obliged to take on.

Order of priority

I enjoy spending time with her.	
I feel it's my duty.	
The family think it's my duty.	
There isn't anyone else who could do it.	
I would feel terribly guilty if I didn't look after her.	
It just seems the right thing to do.	
She won't let anyone else look after her.	
The care home fees are very expensive.	
It's my way of paying her back for the love she gave me.	
I promised I'd never put her in a home.	
I have a strong sense of family. I think families should look after their own.	

Food for thought

For your caring relationship to be successful, it's important that it is something you have chosen, and feel committed to. If your reasons for becoming a carer are mainly negative, or if you feel pressured by other people's wishes rather than your own, you need to consider whether there is someone else who could care for her, or what other caring arrangements would be possible.

Marian

'He said he'd like to live with his daughters, and when he got a good offer for his house, it seemed like the right time. I'd already talked it over with my husband, and he agreed. The original arrangement was that he was going to spend six weeks with my sister and six weeks with me. But it hasn't worked out like that.'

Anne

'We had a lovely childhood, I feel it's giving something back.'

Zahira

'She won't let anyone else touch her. Sometimes we have an argument and she says, 'I'm going to die.' And I say, 'Alright then, die.' But then I see her closing her eyes and I start to cry.'

In conclusion

It would be lovely if there was a simple formula which would produce the right answer for everybody. But everyone's personality and circumstances are so different that, in the end, it is up to each person to decide what is the right way of caring for them, and how long they should go on caring.

The questions above may have helped you to weigh up your own situation. Read through the answers you have made, then try to fill in the statement below.

Caring statement

I would prefer to care for my relative

at a distance ☐   living nearby ☐   as a live-in carer ☐

I am willing to help her with _____

_____

_____

_____

I am not able or willing to help her with

_____

_____

_____

_____

I would like help from

social services ☐   voluntary helpers ☐   paid helpers ☐   my family ☐
with

_____

_____

_____

_____

I can go on caring for her until

_____

_____

_____

_____

Chapter 2 looks at how you can match the care you are willing and able to give to the range of options open to you and your relative.

Marian

'The trouble is, my husband and I aren't getting any younger ... if we don't do things together now, we may not be together as a couple much longer.'

Marian's father is 96 years old and in poor health. He had lived alone for 16 years after his wife died. Four years ago Marian decided that he should come and live with them. She made a decision to give him a couple of years of peace and security at the end of his life. Four years later he's still with her. But now her circumstances have changed, and she feels trapped.

'In that time a lot of things have changed. My husband had a heart attack and took early retirement, and although he's made a good recovery, things are different now. At one point I was having to look after both of them. Now my husband's at home all day, and so is my father. They don't get on. There's no animosity between them, but I can see my husband would like a bit more attention from me; he'd like to have me to himself more.

'Father is quite demanding. I suppose when you're sitting in a chair all day you can become demanding. As far as he's concerned, we're still his little girls. He doesn't realise that I'm in my 60s and my sister is 70.

'One problem is that my father has taken over the sitting room all day so we don't get much privacy. He just sits there. Sometimes he reads the paper, or we talk about the past. It's as though he's just waiting to die. He doesn't like using his toilet bottle in front of us, so we always feel we have to leave the room when he wants to use it, which is quite often. It means we can't feel at home in our own house. Now we've agreed on some regular respite care I feel much better.

'It's the indefiniteness of it that gets me down. It's such an open-ended commitment. If we knew how long he was going to be here we could plan. We'd like to go away on a special holiday together, but we don't really feel we could leave him, even if he went into respite care, in case something happened while we were away. I feel quite trapped. The trouble is, my husband and I aren't getting any younger, and since my husband had his heart attack I keep thinking – if we don't do things together now, we may not be together as a couple much longer.

'If I'd known at the beginning how it was going to work out with my father, I think I might have arranged things differently.'

2 How much care does your relative need?

Some older people can manage quite well so long as they have some basic help around the house. Others have a physical disability which means that they cannot get around or do things for themselves, but their minds are perfectly clear. Yet others may seem physically fit and well, but their mental health has begun to deteriorate, so that they can be a danger to themselves and to others. The kind of help your relative needs will depend on her illness or disability at present, and also on how her health is likely to change in the future.

This chapter is about how you can work out what care your relative needs, how to make the most of the social services assessment system, and how to plan for the future.

Dawn

'At first, I was going round every day and doing everything. But then my doctor showed me how to get help.'

Dawn's mother had been chronically sick with emphysema for years. As she grew older she also suffered from confusion and memory loss. Even though she was confined to her bed a lot of the time, she didn't want to go into a nursing home. Instead she stayed in her own flat, and Dawn cared for her for five years before she died.

'At first, I was going round every day and doing everything. But then my doctor showed me how to get help. He arranged for the district nurse to come regularly to turn her and tend to her pressure sores. Social services came and did an assessment of her needs and arranged for a home care assistant to come in every lunchtime, but later that was increased to the evenings as well. I cooked her meals and froze them, and the home care assistant heated them up for her. She was able to claim Attendance Allowance and also Severe Disablement Allowance and I used the extra money to pay privately for a bath nurse and a cleaner. I found them through an agency. I said to the cleaner, 'I don't mind what you do. I don't mind if you just sit and talk to her' – because it was a time when I knew there was someone with her, and it was a weight off my mind.

'As she became more ill, her character changed, and she was often very aggressive. There were two lovely ladies who lived on the same landing who popped in to see her regularly. I don't know how they put up with her, because as her character changed she was quite nasty to them. She was often nasty to me, too. I used to get very upset, because I was so close to her. The doctor said, 'It isn't your Mum. You've lost your Mum.' I kept hoping my real Mum would come back. But she never did.

'After her last illness, she was very frail, and worried about being on her own. She said, 'I don't want to go back to the flat any more.' The social worker helped me to find a nursing home, but she died three weeks later. It seemed awful, dying like that in a strange place. I'm sure if the right care and support were available she would have preferred to die in her own home.'

Assessing what care your relative needs

Your own assessment

Before you and your relative can make plans for her care, you need to know how much and what kind of care she needs. If your relative mainly needs help with household tasks, she will probably be able to manage in her own home with people coming in to help.

Even if she needs some help with personal care it may be possible for her to manage at home. However, if she might be at risk when she is on her own then the care arrangements you make will have to take this into account. Someone with severe dementia will need almost constant supervision, either in a residential or nursing home or living with a carer. If your relative needs a small amount of nursing care, it may be possible for a district nurse to visit her at home, but if she needs a great deal of care a nursing home might be the best choice.

You and your relative can use the table below to help you decide together about her care needs. Even if you are going to involve social services, it is still a good idea to work out for yourselves what you think her needs are. This will put you in a stronger position to discuss with the social services staff what arrangements they will make and what help they will provide.

What type of care does she need?	*How often does she need care? Weekly or less/ Daily/Several times a day/Constantly*
Help with household tasks, eg	
shopping	
cooking	
cleaning	
laundry	
Help with personal care, eg	
getting up and dressed	
washing and grooming	
bathing or showering	
using the toilet	
eating and drinking	

Help with organising her affairs, eg

collocting her pension

paying bills

filling in forms

Someone to keep an eye on her to make
sure she is not at risk

Someone to sit in while the carer goes out

Someone to look after her while the carer
has a longer break (respite care)

Companionship

Someone to help her go out

Someone to take her on holiday

Nursing care

The social services assessment

Many people are reluctant to approach the social services department when they need help. They may feel that social services are for
'problem families' and that they should be able to cope on their own.
But unless you and your relative are going to pay for – or provide –
all her care yourselves, you will need to call social services in. The
social services department (in Scotland, social services departments
are called social work departments) has a legal duty to assess someone who is substantially and permanently disabled. Social services
must also assess people who appear to need the type of care they
provide or arrange.

Someone from the social services department – it could, for example, be a social worker or an assistant or a specially trained assessor
– will visit your relative at home, or if she is in hospital they will talk
to her on the ward. In some areas, social services departments
arrange for assessments to take place away from the home – per-
haps in a day centre. They will ask questions about your relative's

personal circumstances, her health problems, what help she thinks she needs and what help she is already getting.

Once your relative's needs have been assessed, the social services department will decide whether they can offer help. They do this by comparing her assessed needs with eligibility criteria they have set for different services. If your relative's needs meet the social service department's criteria, then they may ask about her financial situation, so they can work out how much, if anything, she may have to pay towards the costs of services.

Although the idea of being assessed can seem intimidating, many people have said that they find the process very helpful. The person who does the assessment should know all about the services which might be available to help your relative. He or she will be in a good position to give advice and to help you and your relative choose a way of caring that suits everybody. If, during the assessment, your relative is found to also have housing or health needs, the social services department should notify the relevant health and housing bodies. Usually, your relative has to agree to their doing so.

An occupational therapist (OT) may assess your relative to see how well she can manage in her own home, and may make recommendations about changes and adaptations which could make it easier for her to manage. The OT can advise about repairs and alterations to the home, and whether a grant may be available. This may be a separate assessment or part of the full social services assessment. Unfortunately in some areas there may be a long wait for an OT assessment.

There is a summary of the services most local authorities provide on pages 67–69. The services may be provided in your relative's own home, or in your home if she is living with you.

For more *i*nformation

❶ *The Community Care Handbook* (2nd edition), published by Age Concern Books (details on p 120).

i Age Concern England Factsheet 41 *Local authority assessments for community care services.*

The carer's right to an independent assessment

The NHS and Community Care Act 1990 encourages care in the community and acknowledges the important role carers play, and this is reiterated in the Carers (Recognition and Services) Act 1995, which came into effect from April 1996. Care in the community would soon break down without the great army of carers, mostly unpaid, who give their time and effort to making it work. Caring can be difficult and stressful, and for this reason carers are entitled to ask for a separate assessment of what they need in order to continue to care for their relative or friend, or because they can no longer manage to provide any of the care. This applies to carers who provide – or who intend to provide – 'substantial and regular care'. For example, you may be able to continue to care if you have some additional help at home, or respite care, or, if you know this help would be available, you might choose to begin to care for a relative or friend. Many carers also find it helpful to talk to a counsellor or psychiatric nurse about their own feelings and the strains they are under.

You may ask for an assessment at the same time that your relative is assessed. Or you may find after you have been caring for a while that you are having difficulties, and you may then ask the local authority to reassess the situation because it is no longer possible for you to provide some or all of the care. Your assessment as a carer can only take place if the needs of the person you care for are being assessed or reassessed. However, this should not mean that your needs are not assessed separately from that of the person you care for, and you should be able to talk in private, away from the person you are caring for, so that you can talk freely about your difficulties without worrying about upsetting them. Once the assessment of needs has been carried out, the social services department may suggest services which would meet those needs. Carers National Association has more information about assessments for carers.

If you do not agree with the assessment

It may happen that you and your relative are not happy with the services the social services department are offering. Local councils are sometimes not able to offer people all the care they feel they need, and they may not even assess someone as having needs which they know they cannot meet. Or you may feel that they are putting pressure on you and your relative to go along with a way of caring that does not seem to be right for you, and you may have to hold out for what you really want. There is more about how to do this on page 98.

Note Since March 1997, local authorities can take their own resources into account when deciding whether someone has a need for a service under the Chronically Sick and Disabled Persons Act 1970, and which services they will then arrange or provide. Services cannot be withdrawn or reduced until the person's care needs have been assessed (or reassessed) against revised eligibility criteria. Any reduction in, withdrawal of, or refusal to provide services must not leave individuals at severe physical risk.

What is your relative's long-term health prognosis?

It is important to try and find out as much as possible about your relative's illness or disability, and how it is likely to progress. This will allow you to plan ahead and make long-term decisions. A condition involving physical disability, such as a stroke or arthritis, could mean a lot of heavy lifting. Your own size, strength and stamina, and whether there are other people to help you, might be a factor in your decisions about care. On the other hand, caring for someone with a mental illness can put the carer under tremendous emotional pressure, especially as the illness progresses.

Your own or your relative's GP is the best person to talk to about this. Remember, GPs are bound to observe the confidentiality of their patient unless your relative agrees that you should be involved in the discussion, or unless the GP decides that she is so mentally or physically frail that her family need to be consulted.

You may also be able to get advice and information from one of the specialist charities which provide support and information relating to particular illnesses. You will find the addresses of some of the main ones in the back of the book, but your GP or hospital consultant should know if there is one which is relevant to you which is not listed. If your relative has recently been in hospital, the hospital consultant who looked after her should also be able to give you information and advice about her illness or disability.

What will happen in the future?

As your relative's condition changes, this will also affect you as a carer. How quickly is your relative's condition likely to deteriorate? Will there come a point at which you will no longer be able to provide the care she needs? Even a successful caring relationship can come under unendurable pressure. Yet carers who find they can no longer carry on often feel they have failed or they are letting their relative down in some way. You may find it helpful, therefore, to set yourself some clear limits, as these carers have done.

Alison

'The community psychiatric nurse thinks that it's time for her to go into a home. But we think that as long as she knows where she is, we'll keep her at home. If the time comes when she no longer knows where she is, or if we can't cope any more, that's when we'll consider a home.'

Marian

'I feel that if he should ever become incontinent – that's when I won't be able to cope any more. If that happened, I think he would have to go into the nursing home full-time.'

> ### Anne
>
> 'I think the day she looks at us and doesn't know who we are – that's the day I'll let her go into a home. I don't know how I'll face it at the time.'

You might decide, for example:

I won't be able to care for my relative in the same way once she can no longer walk or I won't be able to care for my relative in the same way once she needs to be lifted or I won't be able to cope if my relative becomes incontinent/doubly incontinent or I won't be able to care for my relative in the same way if it puts too much strain on my relationship with my family.

Setting limits to your care does not mean that you will stop caring, but that you will try to find different ways to care.

3 What are the options?

People are sometimes worried that if they do not care for their relative themselves then the only alternative is to 'put her into a home'. In fact there is a whole spectrum of possibilities. Even if your relative can no longer manage in her own home she might be able to manage in a special bungalow or sheltered housing scheme if there is one in your area. Since the NHS and Community Care Act 1990 there has been an emphasis on encouraging older people to live independently, and on providing support in the community.

Care arrangements can be very flexible, with care assistants from social services and from the voluntary or private sectors working alongside members of the family. Some carers have found that there can be quite a gap between the care that is needed and what the local authority is actually able to provide. However, many carers speak very warmly of the support and help they receive from their care assistants.

This chapter looks at who can care for your relative and where, and sets out some options for you and your relative to discuss.

Alison

'Between us we can cope as long as the support services are there … I feel lucky that I'm sharing the care, and I've got some support.

Alison and her sister share the care of their mother, who lives in her own home. She is 79 and suffers from severe dementia following a succession of small strokes, as well as diabetes and thyroid trouble. She can no longer feed, wash or dress herself, and she is incontinent. From 8 to 12 am a home care assistant comes and helps her to get herself up and washed, and prepares her breakfast. Alison or her sister goes over at lunchtime. Then from 3 to 7 pm another home care assistant comes, and after 7 pm another family member comes to help get her ready for bed.

'Between us we can cope, as long as the support services are there. She has eight hours help a day from social services, and one of us gives her lunch and makes sure she's in bed at night. I feel lucky that I'm sharing the care, and I've got some support. Once she's in bed she's safe, because she sleeps well, and she can't get out and wander.

'All the home helps are from a private agency, and it's an excellent service. We haven't been let down yet. They worked out a care package, together with social services, and I just sign each month to say the carers have been.

'She's getting the maximum home care possible, and we've been told that the cost is the same as if she was in a home. I don't think you'd get this level of support in most areas, and we feel we've been very lucky – though we did have to fight to get it.

'She doesn't go to a day centre – and now we've left it too late. But when she was more mobile I got her into a music and movement class at a private home, and she enjoyed that. We've had respite care once or twice, but it's hard to find somewhere suitable now she's not so mobile. But we are going to try a residential home for a couple of weeks this year – it will also give us a better way of judging what long-term care would be like, if we ever felt we couldn't cope.'

Who is there to care for your relative?

It is all too easy as a carer to get so involved in the day-to-day problems of caring that you forget to step back and see whether there is anyone else who could be sharing the care with you, or even taking over altogether. So it may be helpful to start by looking at the other people, both within your family and outside, who may be able to care for your relative.

Involving the family

A good way to begin is to make a list of all the members of your and your relative's family. Don't leave anybody out at this stage. Even family members who live quite a distance away may be able to offer occasional holidays, to give the main carer a break from caring. Older family members may be able to help by providing company and sitting in. Younger family members may be willing to drop in on the way to or from school, or to take on jobs like shopping, cooking and cleaning. People with cars may be able to help with lifts, visits to town, trips and outings. And of course working members of the family, who may be too busy to help with day-to-day care themselves, may be able to contribute financially towards the cost of paid carers.

Next, make a list of all the caring tasks that need to be done. You can use the one on pages 24–25 for a start, but do add any other care needs that your relative has. Make your list quite detailed; for example don't just say 'housework' – list all the separate tasks you can think of.

Matching the names on the first list against the jobs on the second list may sound easy, but families are complicated things, and tensions and disagreements often come out at times of crisis. If people can be persuaded to volunteer for jobs from the list, which they are willing to take on, they will be more committed to making sure the jobs are carried out properly, and they will also be more aware of all the jobs they have *not* taken on. This can be done at a 'family conference' when everyone gets together, or arranged

33

informally by letter and telephone (see pp 83–84 on talking things over). Even if someone cannot take on a job, they can take responsibility for arranging for someone else to do it, and for paying them if necessary. However, do bear in mind that if someone volunteers for a job, they will want to do it to their standards and in their way – and this may not be the way you would do it.

Who else can help?

Some families have dozens of members who will rally round, while others are small or have few resources. If your family is like this, then your relative may come to depend increasingly on help from the local authority or the health authority, or from the private or voluntary sectors.

For full details of the types of service that might be available through these different sources, see pages 67–75.

What is the best place for your relative?

Your relative probably has strong feelings about where she would like to live, and these have to be considered when making plans for the future. But they are not the only factors. If her preference is to live with someone who will care for her, whether it is you or another family member, then the carer's feelings and preferences are just as important. If she would prefer to stay in her own home, then the risks of living independently have to be weighed against the advantages. How much care and what type of care she needs will also affect any decision about where she should live.

Another issue is how much help and support may be available. If your relative wants to stay in her own home, or to move into sheltered housing or another home nearer where you live, or to move in with you, the local authority should be able to offer help.

Local social services departments can provide care workers and other support directly in someone's home. Sometimes alterations and adaptations to the home, such as a stair-lift or a downstairs lavatory or a walk-in shower, can help an older person keep their independence, and a personal alarm can help to reduce risk. However, every local authority differs in what it provides, and some are much more generous than others. In some areas resources are very limited. If your relative wishes to stay at home and may need help from social services, it is important for her to have an assessment (see pp 25–26). You will then see what help the social services department is prepared to offer. (In Scotland social services departments are called social work departments.)

Some of the main options for you and your relative to consider are set out below.

Staying in her own home

This is the option that many older people prefer, and under the NHS and Community Care Act 1990 there is now much more emphasis on finding ways of letting people carry on living at home. It is a suitable option for almost anyone who is not at risk, or who chooses to take a certain degree of risk in order to retain their independence.

Gill

'We live nearby so she can ring us if something goes wrong, or just for a chat. Sometimes she rings two or three times a night about the same thing, but it's better to know she's all right. Last week she rang up one night because she had a nose-bleed. I told her to keep calm and sit down and hold something over her nose, and kept talking to her while my husband jumped out of the bath and raced over.'

If your relative does want to continue in her own home, you will both have to weigh up the advantages and disadvantages. Disadvantages might include loneliness (especially if she is housebound), the risk of hurting herself or putting others in danger, worries that no help will be at hand if she falls ill, and insufficient help from local authority or other sources. However, the risks can often be minimised, and may be outweighed by the advantages of staying in familiar surroundings, retaining her independence, not having the upheaval of moving, and keeping her network of friends and neighbours close by.

For more *i*nformation

ⓘ Age Concern England Factsheet 6 *Finding help at home.*

ⓘ Age Concern England Factsheet 13 *Older home owners: financial help with repairs and adaptations.*

ⓘ The council's housing department should be able to advise about grants for repairs, alterations and adaptations (see pp 49–50).

ⓘ An occupational therapist is the best person to advise about any alterations to the home for someone who has a disability. OTs can be based either in a hospital or in the social services department of your local council.

Sheltered housing

Sheltered or retirement housing schemes are a halfway option for people who would like the security of someone to keep an eye on them but do not need full-time care and want to live independently. They are developments of flats or bungalows specially adapted for the needs of older or disabled people, with a warden either on site or dropping in regularly and usually an alarm system to each flat.

Moving into sheltered housing would thus allow your relative to retain her independence but with less risk because of the presence of the warden and/or alarm system. Being purpose-built, the flat or bungalow would be more convenient and easier to look after. The disadvantages would be leaving familiar surroundings and having the upheaval of having to sell her home and move house.

If your relative is considering a sheltered housing scheme, it is important to check exactly what the warden does and what hours they work as this can vary greatly. Wardens do not usually help with care, but can alert the family, the doctor or the social services department if something goes wrong.

Most sheltered housing schemes offer homes to rent, though there are also some offering homes for sale. Some schemes are council run, some are private, and many are run by housing associations. They are very much in demand, so it is a good idea to check whether there are any places available. The cost of both rental and purchase schemes can vary depending on location and the quality and facilities in each scheme. If your relative's income and savings are below a certain amount she may be able to claim Housing Benefit to cover the rent.

Your relative may choose to look for a sheltered housing scheme near where she lives at present, or she may prefer to move to a scheme near to other family members. It can sometimes be difficult to find sheltered housing exactly where you want.

Abbeyfield houses

Abbeyfield houses are large houses divided into bedsits. They house up to about ten older people and a resident housekeeper. Two cooked meals a day are provided, which means the cost may be a little higher than in ordinary sheltered housing. They are usually most suitable for fairly active and independent people aged over 75, who do not need personal or nursing care, and who want as much independence as possible, but who can no longer manage to run their own household, or who are lonely and looking for companionship. For some people, they offer the best of both worlds, combining privacy and independence with social and practical support. Some Abbeyfield houses now provide extra care for more dependent people. You can get more information about schemes in your area from the Abbeyfield Society (address on p 108).

For more *i*nformation

🛈 Age Concern England Factsheet 2 *Retirement housing for sale.*

🛈 Age Concern England Factsheet 8 *Rented accommodation for older people.*

🛈 *A Buyer's Guide to Retirement Housing*, published by Age Concern Books (details on p 120).

ⓘ The council's housing department should be able to give you information about sheltered housing schemes in your area. (In Northern Ireland the housing department is called the Housing Executive.)

Living nearby

If the person who needs care and the carer live close to each other, this allows the person needing care to live independently while making it easier for the carer to be at hand and to drop in as often as is needed. This option is suitable for older people who want to have their own space and privacy, but who need quite a lot of help and support from their family. Different people achieve this in different ways, for example:

■ The carer moves to a new home near to where their relative lives.

■ The relative moves to a new home near to where the carer lives (this could be an ordinary house or flat, or it could be in a sheltered housing scheme or an Abbeyfield house).

■ The relative moves into a flat or 'granny annexe' attached to the carer's home.

Shirley

'My son and daughter-in-law have bought a large house and are planning to convert part of it into a flat for us. The idea is that we'll be able to help with babysitting, and they'll look after my husband and give me a break from time to time. I was absolutely thrilled when they offered, but I wouldn't have suggested it myself.'

There are different advantages and drawbacks to all these arrangements, and of course the financial implications need to be carefully considered (see pp 43–54).

For more *i*nformation

ⓘ Age Concern England Factsheet 6 *Finding help at home*.

Living with the carer

Sometimes a carer and the person needing care decide that the best way of caring would be for them to live together. This is a very big step – just as big a step as moving into a care home – and needs a great deal of thought if it is to be successful. The carer's 'self-assessment questionnaire' on pages 5–20 might help you to decide whether it is the best option for you.

Living with a carer can be a good arrangement for someone who needs a lot of care or constant supervision. However, it only works when the carer and the person being cared for have a good relationship and can be tolerant of each other's habits. People who have not lived together before may like to try living together on a temporary basis to see how they get on, maybe for a month's 'holiday'. But everyone concerned – the carer, their family, and the person being cared for – must feel sure that they will be able to be honest if they feel the arrangement is not working well.

You and your family may find the arrangement stressful: you may feel you have no privacy and no life of your own. Or your relative may miss her independence, or find friction between you and her difficult to cope with. It is very difficult to say to a relative, especially to a parent, that you do not want to live with them, and saying it may make you feel terribly guilty. In fact people sometimes end up living together simply because the carer does not feel able to say no.

Zahira

'Sometimes when she can't get to the toilet in the night, she just goes on the floor. It's awful to clean up. But we do it because we love her. You don't want anyone else to shout at your Mum, do you?'

For more *i*nformation

i *Caring at Home* by Nancy Kohner, published by the National Extension College (Tel: 01223 316644).

ⓘ Who Cares Now? Caring for an older person by Nancy Kohner and Penny Mares, published by BBC Education, 201 Wood Lane, London W12 7TS.

Residential or nursing home care

Residential or nursing home care is often the best option for an older person who is too frail or ill to live on her own even with regular support from carers coming to her home. For many older people, 'going into a home' may seem to be a last resort. They may worry about the loss of independence and dignity, or they may feel uncomfortable about being cared for by strangers. For the families, too, care in a home may seem to be an admission that they have failed their relative. But there are many homes where the quality of care is excellent, and the residents live full and dignified lives. For some people, a residential or nursing home may be the best or only option – far better than struggling to cope in their own home, or living with an exhausted or resentful carer.

Your local social services department can help you find a care home for your relative, and may help with the cost if your relative's income and savings are below a certain amount (see below). They will help you decide whether this is the best option, and explain the other possibilities. Contact them to ask for an assessment.

If your relative's income is below the weekly cost of the home, and she has savings and capital of £16,000 or less (including the value of her own house), she should get help towards the cost of the fees. However, her home may not be counted as part of her savings if someone else is living there, as explained on pages 55–56. If social services do not think your relative needs residential care, she may have to pay the full cost herself. The social services assessment procedure is described on pages 25–26.

For more *i*nformation

ⓘ Finding and paying for residential and nursing home care, published by Age Concern Books (details on p 117).

ⓘ Age Concern England Factsheet 10 *Local authority charging procedures for residential and nursing home care*.

ℹ Age Concern England Factsheet 29 *Finding residential and nursing home accommodation*.

ℹ Counsel and Care Factsheet *What to look for in a private or voluntary registered home*.

ℹ Counsel and Care (address on p 111) is a voluntary organisation which gives advice and information about voluntary and private care homes. They may be able to help if you have difficulty in finding a place in a home.

ℹ Elderly Accommodation Council (address on p 112) can send you a computerised list of places in private and voluntary homes and sheltered housing in your area and price range.

ℹ GRACE (address on p 112) is a private agency which can advise you about, and help you arrange, all forms of long-term care, including residential and nursing homes, sheltered housing and care at home. They operate mainly in the south of England, and fees range from about £25 to £75. In some areas social services will cover the costs.

4 Some financial and legal considerations

Questions about money often affect people's decisions about care. But the legal and financial implications of different care options can be quite complex, and people may not be fully aware of them when they are making decisions. If your relative is being discharged from hospital into a private nursing home, for example, she may have to pay for her own care.

This chapter helps you find your way through the legal and financial maze. It looks at some of the expenses involved in being a carer, the implications of different care options, what happens to your relative's home in various circumstances, taking over responsibility for your relative's finances, and the way your working life, your pension and your inheritance could be affected.

Bill

'The trouble is, when he died there was no Will ... So there I was, 62 years old, and without a home.'

'I don't know why, but I never got married. I stayed at home with Mum and Dad. As they got older, I found myself looking after them more and more. I didn't mind doing it, because they'd looked after me for all those years. But it was hard. Mum died of cancer, and not long after Dad had a stroke. I looked after him for eight years until he died. I did everything for him, and we got very close, but we never talked about what would happen after he died.

'The trouble is, when he died there was no Will, so all the money that was left was to be divided equally by the children – well, there was not much money, just the house. I have one sister and two brothers. One sister and one brother agreed that I could stay on in the house, but one brother wanted his share of the money straight away because he was having trouble with his business. He got legal advice, and I was told they could force the sale of the house. The worst thing was, he'd never had much to do with Mum and Dad after he left home – he just wanted his share of their savings. I was really upset, but there was nothing I could do. I couldn't afford to buy out his share. So there I was, 62 years old, and without a home.'

The costs of caring

Whichever way of caring you choose, there are bound to be extra expenses you need to budget for, as well as unexpected expenses which take you by surprise and can make quite a big hole in your family income. You may also be entitled to claim some extra benefits and allowances. For information about the benefits you and your relative may be entitled to, see pages 75–81.

If your relative is receiving Income Support or another means-tested benefit, it is important that she spends her income regularly and does not let it mount up. Carers sometimes feel they are being mean when they ask their relative to pay for something, but if her savings mount up to more than £3,000 her benefit will be reduced, and if she has more than £8,000 she will not be entitled to claim benefit at all.

Gill

'We were paying for lots of her expenses. At one point my mother-in-law's savings mounted up, and she got a letter from the DSS telling us she wasn't entitled to Income Support any more. She had to pay back a large amount that they'd overpaid us. It wasn't so much the money – it was the hassle of having to re-apply when her savings had dropped down. Now we make sure she pays for everything and spends her money.'

Paying for care at home

If your relative needs a lot of help or care at home, the social services department may arrange this, following an assessment of her needs (see pp 25–26), but there may be a charge, depending on your relative's income. (Only income and savings in the name of the person who receives the care can be considered.) If social services decide that she is not entitled to help, or to enough help, from them, you may choose to pay for help privately. There is more about arranging care privately or through a voluntary organisation on pages 71–75.

The charges local authorities make for services people receive in their own homes must be 'reasonable', and you have the right to ask the local authority to reduce or waive the charge.

When you are considering whether a charge is 'reasonable' for your relative to pay, consider all the things for which she currently uses her income and savings. This might include food and fuel, and other costs such as insurance and maintaining her home. Contact Age Concern England (address on p 116) for more information on this.

Direct payments

Since April 1997 it has been possible for local authorities to give people money instead of (or as well as) services. These are known as direct payments. Individuals must use this money to organise and buy the care they have been assessed as needing by the local authority. Some services are excluded from direct payments, in particular those services provided by a close relative living in the same household or elsewhere (except in exceptional circumstances).

At present people who are over 65 cannot receive direct payments. If you are the carer of an older person who has been assessed by the local authority as needing care services in their own home, and would prefer to organise and buy it themselves, then please contact Age Concern England.

Caring for someone who lives with you

When someone moves into your home, it is bound to involve extra expense. Even if you do not begrudge the cost, it is easy to have misunderstandings about money because people have different ideas and expectations. Coming to an agreement right from the start about who will pay for what can help avoid bitterness and bad feeling. The following are some of the items that need to be taken into account.

Food

Although older people often have smaller appetites, they may also prefer different foods to other members of the family. This may involve extra cooking and shopping for the carer. Check whether your relative has any special dietary needs, for example for diabetes or weight control. Her GP will be able to give you advice about this, or you can contact the organisation relating to your relative's illness (see list of useful addresses on pp 108–115).

Heating

Keeping the house comfortably warm for your relative could add greatly to your heating bills, especially if she cannot keep warm by moving around. Check with your local council whether you are entitled to a grant for insulating your home. See also Age Concern England Factsheet 1 *Help with heating*.

Transport

If your relative has to make regular visits to the doctor or hospital you may have to pay for taxi fares. If you have no car you could find out whether there is a community transport service in your area, or ask a friend or another family member to help out.

Incontinence supplies and laundry

If your relative is incontinent you can get help and advice from the district nurse, or from a special continence adviser. Some incontinence supplies (pads and sheets) will be supplied free of charge but many carers find that they are not enough and they have to buy more. You may also find that the extra laundry will add to your fuel bills.

Home safety alterations

When your relative comes to live with you, you may need to invest some money in making your home safe, for example by laying fitted carpets instead of loose rugs, replacing trailing wires and flexes with wired in appliances, removing objects with sharp corners or edges, replacing a gas cooker with an electric one or a microwave oven, replacing glass doors with solid ones and glass bath-panels with moulded plastic, replacing light switches with pull cords. Before your relative moves in, it is worth asking for an occupational therapist to visit your home and tell you what needs to be done and what grants might be available (see pp 49–50)

For more about making alterations to your home, see page 48.

Special equipment

Special equipment such as a walking stick or frame, raised toilet seat, grab-rails, a wheelchair, commode, special chair or bed, even a bath or a bed hoist, can make a tremendous difference to you and your relative. However, such items can be very expensive to buy. The social services department, or the hospital where your relative has been treated, or the community health service (through your GP or district nurse) may be able to lend you some items. It is also worth asking the local branch of the Red Cross. Alternatively you can sometimes buy such items secondhand. They may be advertised in a local newspaper or doctor's surgery, or in the Carers National Association magazine, or through a local carers' group or Age Concern organisation.

For more *i*nformation

i Carers National Association Information Sheet 14 *Gadgets and equipment to aid daily living.*

Caring at a distance

Even if your relative lives in her own home and you manage her care from a distance, there will be costs involved. These could include:

- transport to and from your relative's home;
- telephone bills: if you keep in touch with your relative regularly by phone, or if you have to make a lot of calls to social services or the hospital, your telephone bills will quickly mount up;
- extra purchases of food, clothes or presents. Some carers find themselves often taking over little treats and surprises for the person they care for, or doing shopping for her and then not accepting the money for it. Most people who can afford it do not begrudge this expense, but it is still something you need to budget for;
- alterations and adaptations to make your relative's home safer (see below).

Moving house

Whether you are moving to live with or near your relative, or your relative is moving to live with or closer to you, the expense of moving house can be enormous, especially if it involves buying or selling property. Costs vary greatly in different parts of the country, so you will need to get advice from a local estate agent or solicitor, but here are some of the things you will need to budget for:

Removal fees These will depend on the amount of belongings and distance to be moved – it is best to get at least three quotes.

Estate agents' fees Typically between 0.5 and 2 per cent of the value of the property being sold; ask about extras such as advertising, notice board, etc.

Solicitors' fees Some solicitors charge a fixed amount for conveyancing, others have a scale of charges – it is best to get three estimates.

Stamp duty A tax of 1 per cent on the value of the property you are purchasing above £60,000.

Surveyors' fees Usually your building society will insist on a survey and put you in touch with approved surveyors.

The cost of fitting out the new home For example redecoration, new carpets and curtains, telephone reconnection, new kitchen appliances if the old ones don't fit, and new furniture, especially if your relative is moving into a smaller house.

Altering or adapting your relative's home

Whether your relative is staying in her own home or moving to a new home or moving in with you, there may be alterations and adaptations which could make daily life very much easier and safer for her. Central heating, a downstairs toilet, a shower you can walk into, a stair-lift, wider doors for wheelchair access, extra stair-rails and grab-rails, accessible electric points and switches, removing steps or adding ramps – all these can make a tremendous difference to someone's independence. Such alterations are often expensive, but you may be able to get help towards the cost.

If your relative has a disability, the best person to advise about any home alterations is an **occupational therapist** (OT). OTs are trained to look at how people with disabilities can manage everyday tasks, such as getting about, washing, using the toilet, cooking, preparing drinks and eating, and to suggest ways these could be made easier. OTs can be based either in a hospital or in the local social services department and will visit you at home.

In some areas, home improvement agencies (sometimes called Care and Repair or Staying Put) have been set up specially to advise older people and people with disabilities about repairing and adapting their homes. To find out whether there is a branch near you, look in the telephone directory, ask your local housing department, or contact Care and Repair Ltd (address on p 110).

Grants from the council

You or your relative may be able to get a grant from the local council towards the cost of improvements and alterations. This will depend on your or your relative's income and savings and on whether the council has the funds available.

There are two kinds of grant: **mandatory grants** are grants the council has to pay if the work qualifies and a person's income and savings are low. With **discretionary grants** it is up to the council to decide whether to give them or not.

Renovation grants are discretionary grants, and can be paid for essential repairs to make a property structurally safe and habitable, and to provide essential services such as an indoor toilet or a bath or shower with hot and cold water.

Disabled facilities grants may be available to provide facilities for a disabled person. These may be mandatory if they are for specified purposes.

Home repair assistance grants are discretionary grants, available for smaller repairs and alterations (these grants are not available in Scotland). You may also get a home repair assistance grant for alterations to enable a person aged 60 or over to move into a carer's home, such as installing a downstairs toilet. If the work costs more than the amount of grant (a maximum of £2,000 in 1997), you will have to make up the difference yourself.

You should *never* start the work before getting the council's approval to go ahead, or you will not be entitled to a grant.

Can tenants apply for a grant?

Some tenants can apply for a disabled facilities grant, but they need their landlord's permission. Private tenants cannot usually apply for a renovation grant, but the landlord may be able to get one. If the house is in bad repair, tenants should contact the local council's environmental health department. They have the power to make the landlord do essential repairs. Housing association tenants should contact their local or regional office. Council tenants may be able to get a disabled facilities grant but not a renovation grant or home repair assistance grant.

> ### Alison
>
> 'She forgot how to use the light switches, so we invested in a lot of automatic timers that go on and off at set times of day and night. We got safety plugs and plastic corners for all the sharp edges and a baby gate for the bottom of the stairs. We found the baby catalogues at Boots and Mothercare full of helpful ideas. We got a heavy spring on the gate and an automatic closer on the door. That stopped her from wandering because she didn't have the coordination to turn the handle and hold the door open at the same time.'

For more *i*nformation

ⓘ Age Concern England Factsheet 13 *Older home owners: financial help with repairs and adaptations.*

ⓘ Carers National Association Information Sheet 19 *Renovation grants.*

ⓘ **The council** should be able to advise you about renovation grants. If your relative is a tenant, they can advise her landlord about applying. The department which deals with grants is usually the environmental health or housing department (the Housing Executive in Northern Ireland).

Residential or nursing home care

Going into a residential or nursing home can be very costly. Fees range from about £200 to £500 per week, depending on where you live and the amount and type of care you need. Many people can get some help from the DSS and the local authority towards the cost, provided their savings are no more than £16,000. If your relative owns her own house, its value may be counted as part of her assets. This is explained below.

Tony

'My mother was shocked when she heard what the nursing home fees were. She said she'd rather look after my grandfather herself. We were doubtful whether she could cope, but so far it seems to be working out all right. She gets help from the council and she also pays a nurse from an agency to come in once a day.'

Getting help from the local authority

The local authority social services department has to assess anyone who seems to them to need care or who is disabled and decide what level of care they need. If they decide your relative needs residential or nursing home care they will assess her income to see whether she is entitled to help with the cost. They will look at both her income and her capital and savings (assets). If she has assets of £16,000 or less and her weekly income is less than the fees of the home, the local authority will contribute towards the cost of the home.

However, if your relative has assets over £16,000 she will have to pay the full fees until her assets drop down to this amount. If she owns her own house or flat and no one else lives there, the council will take the value of the house or flat into account if your relative is moving into a care home permanently. However, the value of your relative's home may be ignored if someone else is living there, as explained on pages 55–56. It is important that your relative should have a trial period in the home before any permanent decision is made (see p 55).

Can anyone else be asked to pay the cost of care for your relative?

Although in some situations a person's spouse will be asked to contribute towards the cost of their care as a 'liable relative', other family members – children, grandchildren, brothers or sisters – cannot be made to contribute to the cost of a relative's care.

However, if your relative chooses to go into a home which is more expensive than the social services department would usually pay for, then you can make up the difference.

You may also choose to pay for 'extras' such as hairdressing or special outings which are not included in the fees of the home. If your relative is going into a nursing home, essential health services such as specialist nursing, physiotherapy and continence advice (but not continence supplies) should have been identified as health needs in the assessment of her needs; they may then be provided and paid for by the health authority rather than classed as 'extras'. The health authority also has responsibilities to provide health services to residents in residential homes. For those in residential homes, this does include continence supplies.

For more *i*nformation

ⓘ *Finding and paying for residential and nursing home care*, published by Age Concern Books (details on p 117).

ⓘ Age Concern England Factsheet 10 *Local authority charging procedures for residential and nursing home care.*

ⓘ Age Concern England Factsheet 29 *Finding residential or nursing home accommodation.*

Paying for continuing care if someone is discharged from hospital

Your relative may be told that she can be discharged from hospital once her medical condition has stabilised, even though she still needs continuing nursing care. In the past, she would probably have been cared for in a long-stay hospital ward or in an NHS nursing home, but in recent years hospitals have increasingly been closing their long-stay wards and people have moved to live in private residential or nursing homes, which they have to pay for themselves unless they qualify for local authority help (see pp 50–51). In this situation people who thought they had a right to be cared for by the NHS have suddenly found themselves faced with huge bills for private care.

The Government has set out guidelines for health authorities about the types of NHS continuing health care which health authorities (and sometimes GP fundholders) should purchase for people in their area. These guidelines (HSG(95)8) also set out how hospitals and social services departments should handle the discharge from hospital of a patient who will continue to need some care. This includes:

■ an assessment of care needs before the patient is discharged;
■ telling the patient in writing what sorts of care will be needed after discharge;
■ which elements of care the NHS will provide and which will come from social services;
■ what the financial implications will be for the patient.

The guidelines also state that health authorities should take particular care to provide proper recovery and rehabilitation time for older people, so that hospitals do not discharge them too early.

Sometimes the hospital staff or the social worker may put pressure on families to care for their relative themselves, even when the families are very reluctant. There are all kinds of reasons, emotional as well as practical, why someone may not be able to care for a relative. If you do not feel you can care for your relative, you should make this clear to the social worker, so that other arrangements can be made. You may feel guilty about this, but it is better than agreeing to care for her and then caring half-heartedly or backing out.

Your relative should be entitled to NHS nursing care if:

■ her medical needs are complex or unpredictable and she needs to see a doctor or specialist nurse or paramedic once a week or more *or*
■ she routinely needs to use specialist equipment or have a specialist treatment which has to be supervised by a specialist nurse or paramedic *or*
■ her condition is unstable, or she seems to be getting rapidly worse *or*
■ the doctors treating her do not think she has long to live.

If someone being discharged from hospital does not want to go into a residential or nursing home, although the doctors think this is what they need, then they should discuss alternative care arrangements with social services. But social services may make a charge for the 'social care' they provide.

However, the Government has not defined what is meant by complex medical needs, nor where NHS care ends and 'social care' begins; each health authority sets its own criteria for care which the NHS funds, including specialist equipment and therapy services, as well as care which the NHS funds in full. This means that people in different parts of the country may be treated differently.

The Government has said that there will be a review if someone thinks they are unfairly being asked to meet the costs of their own care. If your relative is being discharged from hospital and may have to pay for her own nursing care, even though you think she should be entitled to fully funded NHS care because she meets the health authority's criteria for this care, you are advised to contact the Citizens Advice Bureau, the Community Health Council (Health Council in Scotland) or Age Concern England for advice about the review procedure.

For more *i*nformation

𝒊 Age Concern England Factsheet 37 *Hospital discharge arrangements and NHS continuing health care services.*

𝒊 *NHS Responsibilities for Meeting Continuing Care Health Needs* (HSG(95)8/LAC(95)8), available from Department of Health, PO Box 410, Wetherby LS23 7LN.

𝒊 For people living in Scotland, *NHS Responsibilities for Continuing Health Care* (NHS MEL (1996)), available from the Scottish Office Home and Health Department, St Andrews House, Edinburgh EH1 3DG.

What happens to your relative's home?

If your relative goes into a care home

Someone going into a care home can usually have a 'trial period' first, to see whether they are going to be happy there. Most local authorities allow a trial period of an agreed number of weeks. If your relative normally receives Housing Benefit or Income Support for home commitments, these monies will only continue to be paid for a 'trial' period of up to 13 weeks. During this time, it is important for your relative to keep her options open, and not to give up or sell her own home.

If her stay is going to be permanent, the value of her home may be counted as part of her assets. This will almost always come to more than £16,000, which means that she will be expected to pay the full cost of the care home herself until her assets have dropped down to £16,000.

Note **If your relative goes into a residential or nursing home for a 'temporary' stay – which means that she intends to return either to her own home or to some other form of accommodation such as sheltered housing – she can continue to receive Housing Benefit or Income Support for home commitments for up to 52 weeks.**

Your relative cannot be forced to sell her home, but the local authority can put a legal charge on it. This means that when the property is eventually sold, they have first claim on the proceeds of the sale to pay off the money she owes them.

However, the value of your relative's home must be ignored if there is someone else living there who is:

- a spouse or partner;
- another relative who is aged 60 or over;
- another relative who is aged under 60 but who is disabled.

If someone lives in the property who does not fit into the above categories, for example an older person (over 60) who is not a relative or a younger person who has given up their own home to live with your relative and care for her, the local authority has a discretionary power to ignore the value of the property.

For more *i*nformation

i Age Concern England Factsheet 38 *Treatment of the former home as capital for people in residential and nursing homes.*

Is it possible to protect your relative's assets?

Some people try to get round the savings rule by giving money or property away to family members. However, if the council thinks that this has been done deliberately to avoid paying care home fees they may be entitled to get the money back from the person who gave it away. If it happens within six months of the person going into a care home or while the person is living in a care home, they may be entitled to get the money back from the person it was given to. This is called the **deprivation of assets rule**.

Some families refuse to let an older relative who needs a great deal of care go into a care home, and insist instead that she is looked after in the community with carers coming into the home in order to avoid having to sell her home. However, many local authorities now set a limit to the amount of home care they are willing to provide, for example 14 hours per week. If someone needs – or feels that they need – more care than this, either the local authority will provide this in a care home or the person and/or their family will have to make private arrangements for the extra care at home, which they will have to fund themselves. If you feel unhappy with what the local authority is offering, you can make a complaint, using their complaints procedure.

For more *i*nformation

i Age Concern England Factsheet 40 *Transfer of assets and paying for care in a residential or nursing home.*

If your relative's home is rented

If your relative rents her home, and there is no one else living there, then she will probably have to give up the tenancy once she moves permanently into a care home. In some cases, especially with council houses or flats, it may be possible to assign the tenancy to another member of the family who has been living there. This depends on the policy of your local authority. Your relative should speak to the housing manager if she would like to do this. If she is renting from a private landlord, her rights will depend on how long she has been in the property and what kind of tenancy she has. In this situation, it is best to get advice from a solicitor or a Citizens Advice Bureau.

Living with your relative – what will happen when she dies?

If you are living in the house of the person you care for, you may be worried about where you will live when she dies. If your relative owns the house, she can make arrangements in her Will which allow you to stay.

A son or daughter living with an elderly parent may sometimes find themselves in a difficult situation if there is no Will. According to the law, the property of the deceased must be divided equally between all the children. This means that brothers and sisters of the carer will have equal rights to a share of the property. This can cause great bitterness, especially if the house has to be sold and the son or daughter who has been the carer is left without a home. Although it is not easy to raise the subject of a Will with someone you care for, it may be important for your own peace of mind to know that they have made arrangements for you.

For more *i*nformation

ⓘ DSS booklet D49 *What to Do After a Death*, free from local Benefits Agency (social security) offices.

ⓘ Age Concern England Factsheet 7 *Making your Will*.

ⓘ *Wills and Probate* and *What to Do When Someone Dies*, published by the Consumers' Association, 2 Marylebone Road, London NW1 4DX. Tel: 0171-486 5544.

Taking over responsibility for your relative's affairs

Carers often worry about what will happen if in the future their relative becomes mentally confused, and cannot manage to look after her own affairs. Whether you are caring for her at home or at a distance, or she is in a care home, the important thing is to obtain an enduring power of attorney before your relative becomes mentally confused, to avoid having to apply to the Court of Protection later. This is explained below.

Power of attorney

In England and Wales, power of attorney gives someone the legal right to manage another person's financial affairs. This allows you access to the person's bank and building society accounts and enables you to dispose of their property. An **ordinary power of attorney** becomes invalid if the person giving it becomes mentally incapable of understanding what is happening.

If your relative is becoming increasingly frail or confused and you are worried that she will soon be unable to manage her own affairs, it is best for her to apply for an **enduring power of attorney**. This must be arranged in advance, before your relative has become too confused to give her consent, but will continue to apply after she has become too confused or ill to make decisions for herself.

It may be difficult to raise this subject with your relative. Some people make arrangements for an enduring power of attorney at the same time as they make their Will. They can write in a provision that it will come into effect only if their doctor diagnoses them as being mentally unsound.

As soon as your relative is becoming or has become mentally disordered the enduring power of attorney must be registered with the Public Trustee. At the same time, you should inform your relative and other family members. Once the Public Trustee has registered the document, it will be stamped and sent back. You can then show it to the bank, building society, etc, in order to withdraw money or carry out other transactions. However, there are still rules laid down by the Court of Protection about how the money can be spent.

You can buy a special document to create an enduring power of attorney from a legal stationer, or you can ask a solicitor to draw one up for you. A booklet called *Enduring Power of Attorney*, available free from the Public Trust Office, explains how to go about it. It is important to do this as soon as possible, as it will not be valid if your relative becomes incapable of understanding what she is doing before she or the 'attorneys' have signed it.

The Court of Protection

In England and Wales, if your relative becomes mentally incapable before she has given someone an enduring power of attorney, you may need to apply to the Court of Protection for authorisation to manage her money. If a person has assets of more than £5,000 the Court usually appoints and supervises a **receiver** to manage their affairs. He or she is usually allowed a certain amount of money to cover the person's living expenses, but they have to get permission from the Court to spend more or to carry out other transactions. The receiver has to show the Court receipts for all payments made from the person's money. The Court charges a fee for supervising the receiver.

This is a costly and complicated procedure and it is better to avoid it if you can by encouraging your relative to create an enduring power of attorney in good time. But if you have no choice, you will find it helpful to speak to someone at the Citizens Advice Bureau or see a solicitor.

Managing someone else's affairs in Scotland

Informal arrangements

A legal principle (called **negotiorum gestio**) allows you to act on behalf of an incapable person, providing your actions are for her benefit. It applies when it can be assumed that the person would have authorised you if she had been capable. This principle may be useful in an emergency situation, for example when immediate repairs are required to a house and you need to claim back money spent on someone else's behalf. Some organisations may not accept this informal arrangement.

Power of attorney

If the power of attorney was signed after 1 January 1991 it will remain valid after the person giving it becomes mentally incapable. A solicitor will be needed to prepare the power of attorney.

Curator bonis

If your relative has not appointed a power of attorney and is mentally incapable of looking after her affairs or appointing someone else to look after them, then a **curator bonis** may have to be appointed. A curator bonis is an individual appointed by and responsible to the court. Usually a solicitor or accountant is appointed as curator (though not necessarily) and has to manage all the financial affairs and property of the person. The application to the court for a curator bonis to be appointed is prepared by a solicitor, usually on behalf of a close relative of the person. Having a curator appointed is expensive and any professional will charge an annual administration fee. It is therefore not recommended for people with less than £15,000 of capital.

For more *i*nformation

ⓘ *Dementia: Money and Legal Matters*, available free to carers from Alzheimer Scotland – Action on Dementia (address on p 108).

ⓘ Age Concern Factsheet 22 *Legal arrangements for managing financial affairs*, available from Age Concern Scotland (address on p 116).

i *Information for Families of Persons Subject to Curatory*, free leaflet available from the Accountant of Court (address on p 108).

i *Dementia in the Community*, free leaflet available from the Mental Welfare Commission for Scotland, K Floor, Argyle House, 3 Lady Lawson Street, Edinburgh EH3 9SH.

Collecting State Pension and other benefits

You or another close relative can collect your relative's pension or benefits for her as her agent. If this is a temporary arrangement, she will complete and sign the declaration on the reverse of the pension order each week to enable you to collect the money. If you need to use this method for a long period, an agency card may be obtained from the local Benefits Agency (social security) office.

If your relative is unable to act for herself, for example because of dementia or because of a temporary incapacity, the local Benefits Agency may appoint you to act on your relative's behalf as an appointee. This enables you to make claims for and to receive benefits and to spend them on behalf of the claimant. If your relative is in a residential or nursing home, and a relative or friend does not live close by, then the local authority may recommend someone or the person in charge of the home may be appointed, but only as a last resort.

For more *i*nformation

i To find out more about the **Court of Protection** and the **Public Trust Office**, contact them at the address given on page 111.

i *Enduring Power of Attorney* and *Handbook for Receivers* are available free of charge from the Public Trust Office. Send a large sae to the address on page 111.

i Age Concern England Factsheet 22 *Legal arrangements for managing financial affairs.*

i *Managing Other People's Money*, published by Age Concern Books (details on p 119).

Combining working and caring

Some carers carry on working because they need the money, some because they like their job, some because they need the escape from the daily stresses of caring – or it may be a combination of all these. Whatever your reasons, you are taking on a double burden (more, in fact, if you have family responsibilities as well) and there are bound to be times when you feel you are not giving enough to your job or your family or the person you care for.

If you have a sympathetic employer they will understand your difficulties and try to make flexible arrangements or give you paid or unpaid leave. Some employers, such as Barclays and the Midland Bank, are known for their positive policies towards staff who have caring responsibilities. On the other hand, if your employer is unsympathetic you may be afraid of letting them know of your situation for fear of losing your job. In this case, it is a good idea to ask for advice from your trade union. They will know what your employer's policy is and they may be willing to try to negotiate a deal for carers – not just for you as an individual but for anyone in your situation. They will also be able to advise you of your employment rights. If you are not a member of a union you may still find it helpful to get advice from the union which represents people in your kind of employment. You can find out details by ringing the TUC (address on p 115).

Flexible working arrangements

Working part-time may seem to offer the best of both worlds. However, if you already have a full-time job, going part-time needs a great deal of thought. Your security of employment and conditions of service will be protected under European equal opportunities law, but you may find that your career prospects and position within the company are affected. Although you may still be included in your company's pension scheme, you and your employer will obviously be making much smaller contributions.

Job-sharing is an option which sometimes offers employees a better deal: rather than working a number of hours in a part-time job, you will actually be doing half of a full-time job, which will have its own status. But of course you need to find someone to share your job with, and not all employers are sympathetic to the idea.

If part-time working or job-sharing seems like a good idea, you should approach your employer's personnel or human resources department. At the same time, if there is a trade union in your workplace, you may find they are willing to negotiate on your behalf, and this may make you feel less isolated and vulnerable.

Janet

'When Dad's cancer was diagnosed, I thought I would go part-time so that I could spend more time looking after him. I was manageress of a department in a shop, and the trouble was, going part-time meant I had to go back on the shop floor. I found it very hard. I could see what my manager was doing wrong all the time, and it was all I could do to stop myself criticising. And it's hard having someone half your age telling you what to do when you've been used to having that authority. Although I badly needed the money, I left in the end.'

Your pension and other benefits

If you are thinking of giving up your job or working part-time, you must think not only about how your immediate finances will be affected but also about how they will be affected in the long term. In particular, your pension may be affected if you stop making payments or the payments are reduced. Pension arrangements can be quite complex, and it is wise to get expert advice. The personnel department or the trade union at your workplace or the DSS should be able to help you.

If you give up work to care for your relative, you may be able to get Home Responsibilities Protection to protect your future State Pension rights. Some people get this automatically, but you may need to fill in a special form. To find out more, contact your local Benefits Agency office.

Carers who give up a job to look after someone for 35 or more hours a week may also be able to claim Invalid Care Allowance, provided the person they care for is claiming Attendance Allowance or Disability Living Allowance (the middle or highest level of the care component – see p 79).

Anne

'Sometimes I think I'd really like to leave work, but I can't afford to. We took on a bigger mortgage when we moved up here to be nearer to Mum and Dad. Besides, despite the pressure I sometimes think that going out to work helps to keep me sane. Fortunately my employers, the Midland Bank, are very understanding. We can have up to five days' leave for home responsibilities without losing any pay. If things got worse, I could ask for more. It's at the manager's discretion. Last year, when everything suddenly snowballed and got on top of me, I realised I just couldn't cope. The manager took one look at me and said, 'Go home!' And that was it for two weeks. After that I had a week's holiday, and by then things were sorted out and I was all right. My advice to anyone is, tell your employer if you're looking after somebody. If you approach them in the right way, and they know you're not taking advantage, the chances are they'll be amenable. They have been very good to me, and it's made me feel more committed to them.'

For more *i*nformation

i Age Concern England Factsheet 20 *National Insurance contributions and qualifying for a pension.*

i *The Pensions Handbook*, published annually by Age Concern Books (details on p 119).

i **New Ways to Work** (address on p 113) is an organisation that gives advice to individuals and employers about flexible working arrangements.

ⓘ **The Trades Union Congress** (TUC – address on p 115) gives information about employment rights and trades unions.

ⓘ **The Pensions Advisory Service** (address on p 114) will deal with queries and problems about your pension that you cannot sort out with your employer or pension provider.

5 What help is available for carers?

Many older people and their carers struggle on without the support they need because they do not know what is available in their area, or they do not know how to go about getting help. This chapter looks at some care services which are widely available. However, the range of services offered by local authorities and the fees they charge vary greatly from place to place, so you will need to check with the local social services department which services are available in your relative's area. As well as social services, you may also be able to get help through the health service, or from a voluntary organisation or private agency.

Although we all pay for the welfare state out of our taxes, many people, especially older people, do not like to ask for help. This chapter also sets out some of the main benefits which older or disabled people and their carers can claim, and encourages them to apply.

Gill

'The services may be there, but the problem is getting them. It's finding your way around the system.'

Gill's mother-in-law is 90 years old and has Alzheimer's, but with regular support from her family and social services she is still managing in her own home. Someone drops in from social services every morning to make sure she takes her tablets, but she gets herself up and dressed. She goes to the day centre every day during the week, where she has a hot midday meal. Gill and her family visit and cook for her at weekends and do her shopping, cleaning and laundry.

'It's a family effort. I cook the meals, my husband drives them over. If we're away, our son steps in. Sometimes he goes and fetches her fish and chips. If we don't cook for her, she just eats bread and marmalade. Once we opened her wardrobe and found it was full of cakes and buns we'd brought for her. She hides her dirty washing, too. I suppose she's embarrassed because of the smell. I can't get her in and out of the bath – she weighs 13 stone. She tries to wash herself, but it's not really enough. That's one problem we still have to solve.

'I wouldn't say everything's perfect, and obviously there are crises, but I'm sure she has more happiness and freedom in her own home than she would in a residential home. We've been very fortunate with the help we've had from social services. The lady who gives her her tablets in the morning, or the home help, will ring if they think something's wrong, and the day centre rings if she doesn't turn up. Sometimes we all meet up at her house, but often it's a case of keeping in touch by phone.

'Knowing how the system works and having a good working relationship with all the staff are important. The services may be there, but the problem is getting them. It's finding your way around the system.'

Getting help from social services

As explained on pages 25–26, you can ask the local authority social services department (called social work departments in Scotland) to carry out an assessment of your relative's needs. Once this has been done, they will decide whether they can offer help.

Although any services offered will be organised by the social services department, they may not all be provided by them. Some may be provided by private businesses or by charities such as Age

Concern. The list below describes some of the care services which are available in some parts of the country. If there is a service on the list which you think would be helpful to your relative but is not offered in your area, it is worth asking anyway. Even if you do not get it immediately, the social services department may realise that there is a need for this kind of service.

Alison

'Someone asked me if I was looking forward to Christmas. To be frank, I'm dreading it. All the services disappear, but your need for them doesn't disappear. She doesn't stop wetting the bed just because it's Christmas.'

Help you may be able to get through social services

- Assessment of your relative's needs (see pp 25–26).
- Support and advice from a social worker.
- Help in finding residential or nursing home care if necessary (see pp 40–41).
- Carers coming to the home, for example to help your relative get up and dressed in the morning, to help her get to bed at night, to help her with personal care and bathing, to check up on her at regular intervals, to help with domestic tasks, or to make sure she takes medication regularly.
- Meals on wheels: some local authorities provide this service themselves, but many now buy it in from voluntary organisations.
- Laundry service: very few local authorities now offer this, but it is worth asking.
- Regular care at a day centre: some day centres also offer meals, baths, hairdressing, chiropody, education classes and social activities.
- An occupational therapist to advise about aids and alterations at home.
- Grants towards the cost of repairs and adaptations to people who qualify on income grounds.

■ Respite care: this could be someone coming to sit with your relative while you go out for a few hours; someone to sleep overnight occasionally to give you a good night's sleep; a place where your relative can stay for a week or two while you have a holiday; or another family who will have your relative to stay with them on a regular basis. For more about different types of respite care see pages 101–103.

Note Although many local authorities offer some or all of these services, there may be a long waiting list and there will almost certainly be a charge for some of them. For information about how local authorities charge for services for people living in their own homes, see page 44.

Getting help from the NHS

Most people, when they need medical help or advice, go first to their GP. Then, if necessary, the GP can refer them to a specialist at the hospital. This reflects the way the NHS is organised into two distinct areas: **primary care**, which is based in the community and delivered through the GP, and **specialist care**, which is often based in hospitals. Sometimes services delivered in someone's home can come either through the GP or through the hospital, and this makes it quite difficult to work out who is responsible for what. Listed below are the main community-based and hospital-based services.

Community-based services

■ Health care from the general practitioner (GP), including visits at home if necessary.
■ Nursing at home from the district nurse.
■ Help with incontinence from the district nurse or continence adviser.
■ Visits at home from the community psychiatric nurse.
■ Visits at home from the health visitor, who can advise about other services.

- Help from an interpreter for people whose mother tongue is not English.
- Dental treatment: this can be arranged at home for someone unable to visit a surgery.
- Optician services: again, these can sometimes be arranged at home.
- Chiropody: this is usually free for older people who require chiropody, and there is often a community or mobile service.
- Special equipment, such as bedpan, zimmer frame, wheelchair and other aids: these may be available through the local NHS district nursing or physiotherapy services.

Hospital-based health services

- Specialist treatment from a consultant, and follow-up treatment if necessary.
- Help and advice from a Macmillan nurse if your relative has cancer.
- Help and advice from a specialist nurse, for example a stoma care nurse or a diabetic liaison nurse or a mastectomy counsellor.
- Physiotherapy – at the hospital or at home.
- Speech therapy – at the hospital or at home.
- Home visit from an occupational therapist to prepare your relative for being discharged from hospital.
- Loan of crutches, zimmer frame and other aids.

Note **You may find it useful to have the name and phone number of your relative's GP, and of the district nurse, in case you need to contact them in an emergency, but your relative must agree to this.**

Kim

'What makes me so angry is knowing it didn't have to be like this – if only he'd had the right help at the right time.'

'My father had been fit and healthy all his life, but when he was 85 he had a fall and broke his thigh bone. He was in hospital for eight days. They got him walking with a zimmer frame and crutches, then they discharged him. No one checked who was at home to care for him. There was no preparation, no home visit, no physiotherapy, not even a follow-up outpatient appointment. The GPs at the practice were very nice, but I was shocked to realise that they weren't going to put themselves out at all. They just left it all up to my mother, and she's 85, and quite arthritic herself. She was just shouting at my father, saying 'I told you, they said you'd got to walk.' No one was helping him.

'I rang the GP, and she arranged for a community physiotherapist to call, but that took another three weeks. I arranged for someone from Crossroads to call in every day, to help him with showering and getting dressed. I rang up and sorted out Attendance Allowance for them. I got a wheelchair through the Red Cross. I spent all my spare time on the phone trying to sort things out. Someone from social services did come, but by then I'd arranged what they needed myself.

'But next time I went home I was shocked to see how much he had deteriorated. I called the GP again, and this time they referred him back to the consultant. The consultant was quite concerned. He said any progress my father was going to make in regaining his mobility would be in the first six months. He said he needed to have physiotherapy three times a week. But there was a long waiting list for the hospital physio, and the community physio can only come twice a week. She showed the Crossroads helper how to do some of the exercises with him, and between them they do what they can.

'But he isn't improving. He can still manage with his wheelchair and his walking sticks, but he isn't going to get any better. I think they've come to accept this is how it's going to be. What makes me so angry is knowing it didn't have to be like this – if only he'd had the right help at the right time.'

Getting help from the voluntary sector

There are so many voluntary and charitable groups offering different kinds of care and support that finding out about them all is a job in itself. There are large national organisations such as Age Concern and Crossroads, many of which have local branches, there are regional or citywide groups, and there are small community-based groups providing a service in a particular neighbourhood.

The list below highlights some of the services which voluntary and charitable groups can provide, but of course this varies greatly from area to area, and you will need to find out for yourself what is available in your area. A social worker or community worker or the Citizens Advice Bureau should be able to tell you about local groups offering the kind of help you and your relative need. The local church, Age Concern organisation or Council for Voluntary Service can also be good sources of information.

National organisations

- Information and advice about your entitlement to benefits and services.
- Information and advice about money and legal matters.
- Information and advice about your relative's particular illness or disability.
- Information and advice about residential and nursing homes.
- Newsletters and factsheets.
- Advice and support if you want to make a complaint.
- Campaigning for a better deal.

Local organisations or branches of national organisations

- Day care centres.
- Luncheon clubs.
- Social clubs and activities.
- Sitting service: someone to sit with your relative while you go out for an hour or two.
- Care at home.
- Meals on wheels.
- Help with housework.
- Advocacy schemes.

- Befriending schemes and 'good neighbour' schemes: someone comes to visit your relative regularly and makes friends with her.
- Community transport: volunteers take people shopping or to a day centre or hospital.
- Help for people coming out of hospital.
- Help with holidays, trips and visits.
- Support groups for carers.
- Residential and nursing home care.

It is always worth ringing organisations to find out what services they provide. Your local Age Concern organisation or carers' group should also be able to tell you what is available locally. For a list of organisations that might be useful, see pages 108–115.

Note Although voluntary and charitable groups are non-profit-making, most of them do make a charge for some of the services they provide, to cover their costs and volunteers' expenses.

Getting help privately

For those who can afford it, there is a whole range of services which you can buy privately. Even if you cannot afford full private care, many people choose to 'top up' the care they get from social services with extra help to meet their particular needs. Some people use their Attendance Allowance to buy in extra help or to create more flexibility, for example by using taxis for travel, or having their shopping delivered.

Kim

'I found out through a friend about a private nursing home that had its own hydrotherapy pool. They were quite happy for Dad to go and use it, and it made a great difference to his mobility. They made a charge, but it wasn't very expensive. The hardest thing for me has been finding out what's available – you have to do a lot of detective work.'

> ### Alison
>
> 'We managed to get Mum into a music and movement class at a private home.'

> ### Maria
>
> 'Dad was very fussy about his food, and Mum always cooked exactly what he liked. When she died, he was so helpless he couldn't even boil an egg. He tried meals on wheels, but he didn't like them at all. Then an Indian restaurant opened in the village, and they do a take-out service. To our astonishment, Dad found he had a real taste for Indian food. Now he has a hot Indian meal delivered to his door about three times a week, and he talks about nothing else!'

The list below suggests just some of the private services carers have found helpful.

Help you may be able to buy privately

- Paid carers coming to your relative's home: they can be contacted by word of mouth, by advertising or through an agency.
- Paid domestic help: contact as above.
- Help with shopping: you may find a local shop that will deliver to your relative's home – smaller shops may be more helpful than big supermarkets, but their prices will be higher. Some large supermarkets provide transport for shoppers. Some milkmen deliver items such as dairy products, bread, potatoes and tea.
- Laundry: there are agencies which collect and deliver laundry, or your local launderette may do a service wash if someone is able to take and collect it, but they may not accept very soiled laundry.
- Taxis: some offer a reduced rate for pensioners.
- Take-out meals delivered to your relative's home.
- Nursing care through a nursing agency.

- Physiotherapy or speech therapy through an agency or through the hospital.
- Use of facilities in private residential or nursing homes, for example walk-in showers or special bathing facilities, hydrotherapy pool, etc. Many homes let non-residents use their facilities for a fee, and it may be a first step towards your relative getting used to the idea of a home.
- Care in a residential or nursing home (either long-term or respite care or day care).

For more *i*nformation

ⓘ **The United Kingdom Home Care Association** (address on p 115) can give you information about private organisations providing home care in your area.

Note **Always check whether the local authority might provide services before paying for private care. If some of the services listed above would make all the difference to enabling your relative to live independently at home, then it is important to mention it when your relative's needs are assessed. If she has already been assessed, you can ask for a reassessment as her needs change.**

Financial help – benefits and allowances

There are many different kinds of benefits, and claiming everything you are entitled to can be quite complicated. You do not have to be an expert to claim benefits, but it certainly helps to have someone who is an expert to advise you. The Citizens Advice Bureau (CAB) or another local advice centre is a good place to start. A local carers' group or the local Age Concern organisation may be able to help. Some councils have specially trained staff in the social services department.

Sometimes older people are very proud of their independence, and refuse to claim any benefits. Many older people can still remember the prying questions and humiliating means tests of the postwar National Assistance Board. If your relative is like this, do try to persuade her that she is not asking for charity: she or her husband has probably contributed far more over the years than they will claim back. You could point out that some benefits, like Attendance Allowance, do not depend on a means test, and that by refusing to claim she could also be making things more difficult for her carers. The box below gives you some advice about how to claim.

How to get what you're entitled to from the benefits scheme

- If you are not sure whether there is a benefit you or your relative could claim, explain the situation and ask what help is available.
- If you think you or your relative could be entitled to a benefit but you are not sure, you can always claim anyway – you have nothing to lose.
- Make your claim as soon as possible. Some benefits cannot be backdated before the date when you first claim.
- If you or your relative has been refused a benefit you think you are entitled to, don't be afraid to appeal. Many claims which were unsuccessful at first are granted on appeal.
- Get an 'expert' from an advice centre or CAB to help you make your claim or appeal.

Janet

'After Dad's cancer was diagnosed I decided to give up my job, thinking I would be able to claim Invalid Care Allowance. But my Dad refused to apply for Attendance Allowance. He said he didn't need anything. It was just stubbornness really. The worst of it was, he filled in Mum's Attendance Allowance claim form too, and he put that she didn't need anything, although she had severe rheumatoid arthritis and he had been caring for her for years. He said they were managing perfectly all right. So she was turned down for Attendance Allowance, and I couldn't get Invalid Care Allowance. In the end someone from social services found out what was going on and wrote to the Attendance Allowance office explaining the situation, and then her allowance came through soon enough. But by then it was too late – Mum died shortly after.'

Benefits for people with a disability

Attendance Allowance

This is a weekly allowance paid to people over the age of 65 who become ill or disabled. It is meant to help with the cost of being looked after, though it is up to you how you actually spend the allowance.

To qualify for Attendance Allowance someone must need help with personal care (washing, dressing, eating, going to the toilet, etc), supervision, or to have someone watching over them.

Attendance Allowance is paid at two rates. The lower rate is for people who need care either during the day or at night. The higher rate is for people who need care both during the day and at night.

A person must have been disabled for six months before they can get the allowance, but someone who is terminally ill can be paid it straight away.

Attendance Allowance does not depend on National Insurance contributions. It is not means-tested, so it is not affected by income or savings. There is no tax to pay on it, and it does not affect other social security benefits, but it is taken into account in assessing someone's income for residential or nursing home care.

If your relative is able to claim Attendance Allowance, you as the carer may be able to claim Invalid Care Allowance and/or the carer's premium, paid as part of Income Support (see below).

Many people who would qualify for the allowance do not claim it.

Disability Living Allowance

Disability Living Allowance (DLA) has replaced Attendance Allowance and Mobility Allowance for people who become disabled and claim it before the age of 65. There is a 'care component', paid at three different levels according to how much looking after people need, and a 'mobility component', paid at two different levels according to how much difficulty they have in moving about.

Like Attendance Allowance, DLA does not depend on NI contributions and is not affected by income or savings. It is tax-free, and can be paid on top of other benefits. If your relative claims DLA, you (or the person who cares for your relative) may be able to claim Invalid Care Allowance and/or the carer's premium. (This does not apply if your relative gets only the mobility component or the lower rate of the care component.)

Other benefits your relative may be able to claim

Statutory Sick Pay (SSP) Paid by the employer instead of wages for the first 28 weeks to someone who is too sick or disabled to work.

Incapacity Benefit This replaced Sickness Benefit and Invalidity Benefit from April 1995. It depends on your NI contribution record. It is paid at the short-term lower rate for up to 28 weeks, at the short-term higher rate between 29 and 52 weeks, and at the long-term (highest) rate from 53 weeks. The two higher rates of Incapacity Benefit are taxable (though not for people who were already claiming Invalidity Benefit). It cannot be claimed by people over 65, who have to draw their retirement pension instead, but people already over 65 on 13 April 1995 can carry on claiming for a further five years.

Severe Disablement Allowance For people of working age who are too sick or disabled to work but who cannot claim Incapacity Benefit because they have not paid enough NI contributions.

Disability Working Allowance For people with disabilities who are employed but are only able to earn low wages because of their disability.

Industrial Injuries Disablement Benefit An extra allowance for people who become sick or injured through their work. People who contracted an industrial disease before 5 July 1948 may qualify for pneumoconiosis, byssinosis and miscellaneous disease benefits.

Constant Attendance Allowance A weekly allowance for people very severely disabled through their work or a war injury.

For more *i*nformation

❶ *Your Rights*, published annually by Age Concern Books (details on p 119), is a comprehensive guide to money benefits for older people.

❶ DSS leaflet FB 2 *Which Benefit?* explains most benefits and tells you how to claim.

Benefits for carers

Invalid Care Allowance

Invalid Care Allowance (ICA) is the only benefit specially for carers. It is for people of working age who cannot work full-time because they are looking after someone. You may qualify for ICA if you meet the following conditions:

■ You look after your relative for at least 35 hours a week (including evenings, nights and weekends).

■ You do not earn more than a certain amount (£38.70 a week in 1998–99, plus £23.15 for an adult dependant, depending on their income.)

■ You are aged below 65 when you first claim.

■ Your relative receives Attendance Allowance, the higher or middle levels of the care component of Disability Living Allowance, or Constant Attendance Allowance.

ICA is not paid on top of most other benefits. It is counted as income if you are getting a means-tested benefit such as Income Support, Housing Benefit or Council Tax Benefit. But it may still be worth claiming, as it entitles you to the carer premium, paid with these benefits (see below).

Note **If your relative receives the severe disability premium with Income Support, Council Tax Benefit or Housing Benefit, she will lose this if you claim Invalid Care Allowance for yourself. If in doubt, ask the Citizens Advice Bureau to calculate whether it makes sense for you to claim.**

The carer premium

This is an extra amount of money paid to a carer who is getting Income Support, Housing Benefit or Council Tax Benefit. You will be entitled to the carer premium if you are entitled to Invalid Care Allowance (even if you don't get ICA because you are already getting other benefits).

For more *i*nformation

❻ DSS leaflet FB 31 *Caring for Someone?* describes benefits for carers and for disabled people.

❻ Carers National Association Information Sheet 4 *Benefits*, Information Sheet 3 *Carer Premium* and Information Sheet 10 *Invalid Care Allowance*. Send a large sae to the address on page 110.

Benefits for people with low incomes

You may be able to get other benefits or help with costs if you or the person you care for is on a low income. These are summarised below. You can get more information about specific benefits from the freeline numbers and leaflets listed at the end of this section.

Income Support For anyone aged 18 or over who has no more than £8,000 savings, whose income is below a certain amount and who works less than 16 hours a week. (The capital rules are different for people living in care homes.)

Housing Benefit Help with the cost of rent for people on Income Support or a low income and with no more than £16,000 savings.

Council Tax Benefit Help with the Council Tax (called rates in Northern Ireland) for people on Income Support or a low income and with no more than £16,000 savings.

The Social Fund Makes lump-sum payments in the form of a grant or loan to help people on low incomes with exceptional expenses.

Free prescriptions, dental treatment, eye tests and vouchers for glasses There are different rules for different NHS treatments.

People on Income Support or low incomes may be entitled to treatment free or at a reduced cost, as may people with certain conditions or disabilities. Ask your doctor, dentist or optician, or get hold of the Benefits Agency booklet *Help with Health Costs*.

For more *i*nformation

ℹ Age Concern England Factsheet 25 *Income Support and the Social Fund*.

ℹ Age Concern England Factsheet 17 *Housing Benefit and Council Tax Benefit*.

ℹ Age Concern England Factsheet 21 *The Council Tax and older people*.

ℹ Age Concern England Factsheet 5 *Dental care in retirement*.

ℹ **The Benefits Enquiry Line** (0800 88 22 00) for free and confidential advice about benefits for people with disabilities and their carers. Advisers can go through a claim form over the phone and help you or your relative fill it in.

6 Talking it over

When someone in a family needs care, making decisions about who will care for them and where they will live can put the whole family under a good deal of stress. Relationships between parents and children, husbands and wives, brothers and sisters, may all be tested to the limit. Every family is different. Some families pull together at times of stress – in others a great deal of unresolved bitterness and anger can come to the surface.

There is no simple formula for reaching agreement, but there are ways of resolving conflicts without leaving a legacy of bad feeling This chapter looks at some of the difficulties that can arise, and ways of avoiding them.

Kim

'It was a hard time for the family ... But it has also brought us much closer together.'

'My father was such a fit and healthy man, it came as a real shock when he fell and broke his hip. When he came out of hospital he found it hard to walk. No one had asked him who would be at home to look after him, and I hadn't realised how hard my mother would find it to manage on her own. I rang her one day, and she was almost in tears. She said my father was walking less and less, and she didn't know what to do. I went over as soon as I could and sorted out a few practical things. And I contacted my brother and two sisters, to work out how we could help.

'We've all taken on different roles, and it works out really well. My brother lives nearby, and he drops in for a short time every day. My older sister goes for a day midweek. My younger sister lives in Cleveland, so she doesn't see them so much, but she does a lot. She's taken over responsibility for the financial side of things, and she'll go and spend a week with them at half-term. I live about 100 miles away and I have a full-time job, so I go over for one long weekend every month, and a week in the holidays.

'It started off as a practical arrangement, largely because of where we all live, but it's developed beyond that. It was a hard time for the family, and it really put a lot of pressure on all the relationships between us. But it has also brought us much closer together.'

Involving the whole family

Whether you live in a large extended family, or there are just two or three of you, reaching decisions in a way that does not upset or exclude anyone is worth the effort. We all know from experience that sometimes when we are told to do something we may react by digging our heels in or finding reasons for not doing it; whereas if we decide for ourselves that we want to do something, we are much more likely to stick with that decision. The same applies to caring. If everybody feels involved, and feels that the decisions made are really theirs, they will be more committed to making sure things work out for the best. If people feel they have been pressured into something they don't really want, they may not be very motivated to make a success of it.

So the first thing is to make sure that everyone who will be affected by the decision has their say. Your brothers and sisters, if you have any, may have had a very different relationship with your relative, and so have different views about her care. This does not mean that everyone has to agree, or that everybody will get what they want. The important thing is that everybody's needs and wishes are taken into account.

Zahira

'We're a big family – there's about 20 of us who live close by, and we all give a hand caring for Grandma. We're all involved – even the little kids go up and sit with her and she tells them stories about the olden days. We have a rota for who's going to be with her at night. In the daytime I often sit and massage her feet, and tell her what I've been doing. She really likes that. Everyone takes a turn to be with her.'

Whatever caring role you take on, your partner and your children will also be affected. Even if you do most of the day-to-day caring, you may expect them to help, or to take on household chores that have previously been done by you. It is only fair that their views are heard too.

Norah

'It was my decision, and though my husband has been very supportive, I don't feel I can ask him to help. It wouldn't be fair.'

Some families hold a 'family conference' where everyone sits round and discusses plans for the future – it may be at a time when people get together anyway, such as at Christmas or a wedding anniversary. But more often, especially where families are dispersed, people keep in touch informally by phone. This works just as well, provided no one is left out. The situation to avoid is where one family member makes all the decisions, and then informs everyone else.

Maria

'My sister is terribly bossy. She just went ahead and organised everything and gave me this bit of paper to sign. I didn't agree with the arrangements, but I didn't say anything because it would have upset Mum even more, so I just went along with it. It's left a great deal of bitterness between us.'

Muddles and misunderstanding

Listening to others is very important if you are to avoid misunderstandings when you are deciding about care. A good listener is someone who gives us room to say what we really mean without feeling guilty or ashamed. Carers are often very skilled listeners – it is a skill they develop in responding to the person they care for. Listening does not just mean hearing what someone says: it also means hearing what they *don't* say, as in the examples below.

What your relative may think but not say

- 'I don't really like this suggestion, but I'm going along with it because I don't want to upset anyone.'
- 'They're so busy with their own lives – I'm afraid they'll forget about me unless I make a fuss.'
- 'I don't understand what's happening, so I'll just agree with what they say.'
- 'They don't really want me. They're just trying to get rid of me.'
- 'They all want different things. I must try to keep them all happy.'
- 'I'm not going to admit to my illness – then it might not happen.'
- 'They're all ganging up against me.'
- 'I'm the parent – they can't boss me about.'
- 'I'm fed up and angry at being ill. I'm fed up with putting a brave face on it.'
- 'I'm going to die soon anyway, so what does it matter?'
- 'I'm scared.'

What your partner may think but not say

- 'I never really got on with my mother/father-in-law.'
- 'You care about her more than you do about me.'
- 'I want us to do things together without her being there all the time.'
- 'I need to be loved and looked after too.'

What you or your brothers or sisters may think but not say

- 'You were always the favourite.'
- 'You got more attention as a child, so you can do most of the looking after now.'
- 'They always thought you were the bee's knees, but I'm the one that's here when they need me.'
- 'I've always been closer to Mum/Dad. I know what s/he really wants.'
- 'I feel guilty that I'm not doing more for my parents.'
- 'I'm the only one in the family who knows how to sort this out.'
- 'I love my parents, but they're not my priority.'
- 'I just don't think I could cope.'

What your children may think but not say

- 'I don't like Gran/Grandad. S/he's scary.'
- 'She smells funny and she does strange things. She makes me uncomfortable.'
- 'She goes on about boring things all the time.'
- 'I want to be with my friends, not with old people.'
- 'If my friends find out what she's like they'll laugh at me.'
- 'If she comes to live here she'll have the best room.'
- 'I want Mum to listen to me and look after me and give me all her attention, like other people's Mums.'

We often find it difficult to say what we really think. It is often much easier to say what we think others expect to hear, as these examples show. Sometimes it is easier for an outsider to 'hear' the things which are not being said, and to put someone's point of view more clearly than they can. For example, a social worker might be able to explain, 'I think what your Dad is really worried about is that if he accepts respite care it will be the first step towards going into a home permanently.' Or the district nurse might be able to say, 'I know how you feel. Not everyone can cope with incontinence.'

If you feel there is a communication problem in your family, it is a good idea to ask a professional worker, such as your GP or the district nurse or a social worker, to help. They have probably seen many situations like yours before, so they will not pass judgement, and because they are not personally involved they may be able to put things across in a less emotional way.

Reaching an agreement

So long as your relative wants to carry on living at home, most people will agree that this is the best place for her. But if she seems to be at risk, or she wants to move, then you will need to start thinking of other arrangements – and this is where disagreements can arise. Would she be able to stay at home if she got more help? Should she live with you, or another family member? Is a residential or nursing home the best place for her? Feelings can run very high.

Robert

'When it was clear that mother couldn't manage on her own, my sister and I started to look around for a residential home. But our brother was very against the idea of a residential home, and wanted her to carry on living at home. We had terrible disagreements, and all the time mother was getting worse and worse. In the end, when it became clear she did need residential care, her dementia had progressed so much that it was difficult to find a residential home that would accept her.'

The best way to prevent differences of opinion from growing into conflicts is to work towards a consensus – that is, a solution which everyone agrees to, rather than a result where some people 'win' the argument and others 'lose'. In a 'win/lose' argument, nobody likes losing, so people will go all out to defend their position, sometimes even when they can see it is not very sensible or practical. Unfortunately winning the argument can sometimes become more important than finding the best solution for your relative. The end result can be a lot of anger and bad feeling. When people are working towards a consensus, on the other hand, they are more willing to consider different ideas.

Derek

'After Dad got ill he couldn't manage the stairs any more. Mum wanted to move to a bungalow, but Dad wanted to stay put. My brother and I both agreed with Mum, because we could see what a struggle it was for her in that house. We tried to persuade Dad but he just got more stubborn. He said we were all against him. In the end they found a place they both liked.'

Brainstorming a range of different options and going through them one by one is more helpful than starting from fixed positions. When you're trying to reach a consensus, questions like 'What do you think … ?' are a better starting point than statements like 'What I think is …'

It may be helpful to start discussion by finding some basic things you all agree on, for example:

- Your relative's happiness is the main factor in the decision, but it should not override other people's happiness.
- Everyone will do what they can to help, but no one should be expected to give more care than they feel able or willing to give.

Saying the unsayable

Maria

'After Mum died Dad said, 'Haven't you got a little room somewhere where you could fit me in?' I felt my heart miss a beat. I just wanted to run away, but I said, 'Look, Dad, you know we have done nothing but quarrel over the years. What makes you think it would be any different now?' He didn't say anything, and he never mentioned it again. I felt dreadful, but I knew I'd said the right thing.'

Gill

'I said, 'Our son's running his business from home, and he uses the spare room as an office.' That was the truth. What I couldn't really say was that even if we'd had a ten-roomed house I still couldn't have lived with her. We just don't get on. That doesn't mean I don't love her and care for her – in fact I organise my whole life around caring for her. But I need to be able to escape back to my own place.'

One of the hardest things a carer sometimes has to do is to tell the person they care for that they don't want to live with them. Saying 'I don't want to live with you' can seem so impossible that people agree to arrangements they know will not work.

Hilary

'I just couldn't tell her to her face that I didn't want her to live with us. She's been here five years now, and although we've all done our best the strain is really showing.'

The self-assessment section on pages 5–20 may help you to get clear in your own mind whether living with your relative is the best arrangement for both of you. If you know that living with your relative will make you or your family unhappy, then it is better to find another way of caring. Some carers find they can say directly that they would prefer their relative to live somewhere else, others resort to a white lie. Neither way is easy, and you will probably feel very guilty. But committing yourself to something which could be distressing for you and your family is not the answer if the end result is that your relative feels unwelcome and unloved.

For more *i*nformation

ℹ️ *Getting to Yes: Negotiating an agreement without giving in* by Roger Fisher and William Ury, published by Business Books Ltd. A useful guide to solving disputes in a positive way.

ℹ️ **Relate** (address on p 114) can help with all kinds of family conflicts, not just in marriage. Their local address will be in your telephone directory.

ℹ️ **The British Association for Counselling** (address on p 109) can put you in touch with counsellors in your area who can help you solve interpersonal problems.

ℹ️ **Mediation UK** (address on p 113) can put you in touch with local mediation schemes.

7 Making it work

Caring for someone can be a very stressful and difficult experience. It can also be immensely rewarding and satisfying. Everyone has times when they feel they have had enough, but if you feel very negative about your caring role most of the time, maybe you should not be caring at all, or you should be caring in a different way, or maybe you just need a lot more help and support.

This chapter looks at how you can make the most of your caring role and how you can build good working relationships with the other professional workers involved in caring for your relative. It explains how to complain if things go wrong. Finally, it looks at some of the factors which carers say are important to them in helping them to survive and enjoy being a carer.

Norah

'It wasn't guilt or a feeling of duty that made me care for her – it was because I wanted to. And I've enjoyed every minute.'

'Mum is 93 and has been living with me and my husband and two grown-up daughters for three years. She has severe dementia, and no longer recognises us. She came over here for a month's holiday, and I was shocked at how little she could do for herself. I didn't want to let her go home – I wanted to look after her. My husband said, 'If you want your mother to live with us, I don't mind.' We have plenty of room in the house because most of the children have left. She can have a separate sitting room, and my husband and I can be alone together if we need to. She respects our privacy. Once a month she goes to stay with another family under the family placement scheme. They really like her and spoil her, and it gives us a break.

'She doesn't know who we are. She calls my husband Sir. To me, she says, 'I don't know who you are, but you're very kind.' Just because she doesn't know who I am doesn't mean I don't love her.

'My sister thought Mum should go into a home, but I decided I wanted to look after her. My sister doesn't help very much, and sometimes I resent that, but I don't blame her. Her relationship with mother was different to mine – she was the oldest and they were very strict with her. They were both rather domineering types. Also my sister's circumstances are very different to mine. She's a widow and she lives in a small flat. She says, 'I know if I lived with Mum I'd start to resent her.' And I think she's right. She's been straight and honest about her feelings and I respect her decision.

'But I can't forget that Mum helped me with each of my seven babies. She was there when I needed her. So when she needed my help I decided to put my own life on hold. It wasn't guilt or a feeling of duty that made me care for her – it was because I wanted to. And I've enjoyed every minute.'

Dealing with professionals

Care in the community works best when there is a good partnership between the family carers and the professionals such as the nurses, doctors, social workers, home care assistants and other workers who arrange or provide care for your relative. Carers have very mixed experiences of these professionals.

Susannah

'I used to think doctors were gods. I believed in them absolutely. If the doctor had told me to go home and bang my head against the wall six times, I would have done. All that's changed now. I realise they can make mistakes like anybody else.'

Janet

'The district nurse, Fazia, was the first person who really helped us. When she came in through the door, Mum burst into tears. 'We've needed you so much!'

A sympathetic professional can open many doors for you, and help you survive the most difficult times. A lazy or indifferent person can leave you screaming with frustration. Often it is not so much the job they do as their attitude and kindness which make some professionals worth their weight in gold.

Jim

'Getting her across town to the hospital was a nightmare. It was a long walk, and then two buses. It took an hour and a half each way. But the consultant at the hospital was wonderful. When he heard the difficulties we were having he sent a car to fetch us and bring us back. He made us feel so special. He said, "You're the carers and we have to care for you."'

Finding the right person and building a good relationship is the key to survival for many carers. But if you are not lucky enough to come across one of these specially caring workers, there is still much you can do to build a good relationship with the professionals involved in your relative's care.

Communicating effectively

The secret of effective communication is to make contact with the human being behind the official or professional face. This sounds simple, but if you are talking to an overbearing hospital consultant, or a rude council official, remembering that they are only human may take the patience of a saint. However, these pointers may help:

■ Be polite. However much you may feel like it, losing your temper will do more harm than good.

■ Don't treat the other person as an 'enemy' even if they seem to be very negative or hostile. Let them know you appreciate the job they are doing.

■ Try to see things from their point of view and find out what the main issues are for them. Try to find the common ground you can agree about.

■ Be brief. We all tend to ramble when we are nervous, but other people may find it hard to follow our thoughts.

■ Emphasise your main points clearly. It can be hard for the other person to separate out the things which are really worrying you, and the things you are just saying to make conversation.

■ If you are communicating by telephone, make sure you have a pencil and paper handy before you ring, and make a note of the name and extension number of everyone you talk to. In a large organisation, it is all too easy to get passed from pillar to post. Make sure you have got through to the right person before you start on a detailed explanation of the reason for your call.

■ If you are communicating by letter, check that you are writing to the right person, make clear in the first sentence what your letter is about, be as brief as possible, and state clearly what outcome you would like. Don't forget to keep a copy. If you receive no reply to your letter, follow it up with a telephone call.

■ Remember that it may not be your fault if you have difficulty communicating. Some professionals are very poor communicators. Don't be afraid to ask them to explain if you don't understand what they are saying.

Hilary

'Sometimes I don't understand what the social worker's talking about. He keeps going on about 'overarching needs' or 'compensatory behaviour'. I've got no idea what he means. I just nod and say yes.'

Asking for information

One of the things many carers find most difficult is getting the information they need. Whether you want to know more about what benefits you are entitled to or what care services are available, or whether you want to find out more about your relative's medical condition, it's important not to let yourself be fobbed off. These three pointers may help you find out what you need to know:

- Be persistent. If you receive no satisfactory answer, ask again. And again. You may feel a bit like a scratched record going round and round in the same groove, but you will eventually get an answer.
- Ask 'open' questions (eg 'Can you tell me what benefits I might be entitled to?') rather than 'closed' questions, which simply lend themselves to a yes/no answer (eg 'Am I entitled to Invalid Care Allowance?').
- If someone cannot give you the information you are asking for, ask them where you can find out.

Alison

'Nobody tells you anything. It took me weeks to discover I could actually buy extra incontinence pads myself. We found out everything the hard way.'

Making the most of meetings

Meeting with professionals can be nerve-racking. It may seem as though they hold all the cards, and that you have no control over what happens. Some professional workers are aware of this and try their best to make you feel at ease, but even if they do not, these pointers can help you feel more confident.

Arranging the meeting

■ Make sure you know where the meeting is, and that the place and time are convenient to you. If you would prefer to meet in your own home, do not be afraid to say so. If you have to go to their workplace, or you prefer to talk away from your relative, make sure that you will be able to talk in private.

■ Check that you know what the meeting is about. If you would like to put anything else on the agenda, let them know in advance.

■ Ask who else, if anybody, will be there. If you would like to bring someone with you, say so when you arrange the meeting.

■ Talk to the person you care for, if they are not going to be there, and write down a list of their questions and concerns.

■ Be prepared. We have all found ourselves in the situation of coming out of a meeting and realising that there is an important point we forgot to raise. It's a good idea to make a list of all the things you want to talk about, and tick them off as you go along.

Susannah

'The thing that made all the difference was having those two consultants come and visit us at home, and talk to me as if I was an intelligent and responsible person. I can't describe what a difference it made. It gave me so much confidence in myself. I thought, if they can treat me like an equal, why can't the others?'

During the meeting

■ If it is a large meeting, make sure you know who everyone is, and what their roles are.

■ Listen carefully, and take notes. If there's anything you don't understand, ask people to explain.

- If you have any suggestions or requests, raise them and ask people if they can see any obstacles.
- Ask people for their suggestions, and explain if you have any objections to them. Try to work towards a solution that is acceptable to both of you.
- Try to be aware of any 'hidden agendas' that are influencing the discussion, for example an overstretched budget or disagreements between different departments. You may be able to find out more by asking, 'Are you under a lot of pressure at the moment?' 'Are you having to make a lot of cuts?' etc.
- Be firm about the things that matter to you, but flexible about ways of achieving them.
- Some useful phrases:

  'I know you want the best for my mother/father/mother-in-law/father-in-law, etc ...'

  'What alternatives would you be prepared to consider?'

  'Can you give me time to think about it?'

  'I'm afraid I just can't accept that. There must be another solution.'

  'Can we try it out on a trial basis? And if it doesn't work we can look for another solution.'

  'I know it's not your fault this has happened. But will you help to ...'

At the end of the meeting

- Look at the list of points you made before the meeting, and check that they have all been covered.
- Check that you are clear what has been agreed: *who* will do *what* by *when*.
- Try to end the meeting on a friendly note and thank the others for their time.
- Make a note of the date of the meeting, and what was agreed. (It's a good idea to keep a diary, see p 104.) Then, if there are long delays, you can ring up and find out what's happening.

If things go wrong

If things go wrong, or you're not satisfied with some aspect of your relative's care, it's best to raise the matter directly with the person concerned, or their immediate superior. Try to say what you think is wrong without getting angry or laying blame on them. Remember, the point is to get things changed, not to get things off your chest! However, if the matter is very serious, or you feel you are getting nowhere, do not be afraid to make a formal complaint.

Complaints about a council department (eg social services, housing)

To complain about the way you have been treated by a council department, ask for the person in charge of the section and ask what their complaints procedure is. All social services departments are required by law to have a complaints procedure. Other departments will tell you who to write to with your complaint.

If you get no satisfaction, you can write to your local councillor or visit them at their 'surgery' (you can find out their address, telephone number and dates of surgeries from the council offices or the local library). Serious or unresolved complaints can be taken up with the Local Government Ombudsman (look in the telephone directory under Ombudsman).

How to change your social worker

Contact the team leader for your social services area (you can find out their name and telephone number by ringing the main social services number). Explain why you don't get on with your social worker, and ask to be transferred to someone else. The team leader may try to resolve the problem between you and your social worker or agree to transfer you.

Complaints about the National Health Service

It is advisable to approach the Community Health Council (Health Council in Scotland) if you want to complain about some aspect of your relative's treatment or care. They may help you to pursue your complaint through the right channels, or help you with drafting letters. They act as the patient's watchdog in the NHS, representing patients' interests and views.

In the first instance, complaints about hospital care can be taken up with the consultant concerned or with the ward sister, or they can be raised with the hospital's Chief Executive (sometimes called the General Manager).

How to change your GP

Many carers are very appreciative of the excellent service provided by their GP, but some have worrying stories of neglect and indifference.

To change your GP, simply find another GP and contact their surgery to check that they are willing to take you on to their list. You don't have to give a reason why you want to change, and you don't have to tell your old doctor that you want to change. If the new doctor will accept you, your notes will automatically transfer once you have signed on at the new practice. If you do have your NHS card, it is helpful to take it along with you when you sign on at the new practice, but this is not essential.

Consult the local Community Health Council if you need assistance with changing your GP.

Note **Many doctors now work in group practices, so if you prefer you can just ask to see another doctor in the same practice next time you go. Many people do this, and you do not have to give a reason. Just ask the receptionist to make you an appointment with the doctor you want to see.**

Anne

'The GP always made us feel as though we were wasting her time when we said that Mother was drowsy and confused and seemed to be deteriorating. Then we discovered that she had been taking far too many pills. The GP had just issued repeat prescriptions, without bothering to check how many she had had already.'

Kim

'My advice to people is to demand much more from their GP. He or she can arrange all kinds of help, but sometimes they don't bother.'

How to try to change your hospital consultant

Explain to your GP why you are not happy with the hospital consultant, and ask if it is possible to be referred to someone else. If you know the name of a consultant you would like to be referred to, ask your GP if this is possible.

Complaints about private medical care

If you have seen a doctor privately, and have a serious complaint about your treatment, you will need to see a solicitor to discuss whether you should take legal action. The Community Health Council (Health Council in Scotland) cannot help with complaints about private medicine. Complaints about professional misconduct may be able to be addressed by the General Medical Council.

Secrets of successful caring

Every carer will have days when they feel like screaming, but there are a number of factors which seem to make for a more successful caring relationship.

Choosing your way of caring

Carers who have made a definite choice about caring tend to be happier with their situation than people who feel they had no choice, either because of their circumstances or because they were put under pressure to care for someone.

Norah

'I didn't have to care for my mother – it was my choice, and I think that's why it's worked for me. People say to me, 'At least you'll be able to feel you've done your duty by her.' But I didn't do it out of duty. I did it because I wanted to.'

Zahira

'She was the best mother in the world, and now it's our turn to look after her. She was our mother, and now she's become like our child.'

Getting enough respite care

However much you love the person you care for, everyone needs a break from caring from time to time, particularly if you are living with the person you care for. It's not just a break from the exhausting routine jobs you do, it's also a break from the emotional intensity that can build up when two people spend so much time together.

There are many different forms of respite care, and it is worth checking which are available in your area, for example:

Day centres Your relative may be able to attend a day centre once a week or more, to give you time to yourself during the day. Day centres are run by social services and also by voluntary organisations such as Age Concern.

Sitting services Someone comes to your home and sits with your relative, giving you the opportunity to go out.

Overnight schemes Someone comes and stays with your relative overnight, to give you the chance to catch up on sleep.

Family placement or 'home from home' schemes. Your relative goes to spend a few days or a couple of weeks with another family.

Respite care in a residential or nursing home or hospital This may be just once or twice a year, to give you a chance to go on holiday, or it may be part of a regular pattern of care, for example one week in four.

Marian

'We had someone come to the house to sit with him while I went out. The trouble was, I then felt as though I had to go out, whether I wanted to or not. I couldn't relax in my own home. Now he goes into a nursing home two weeks in eight. He doesn't really like it. He doesn't mix with anybody – he just stays in his room. He says, 'It's not like home.' But it helps me to survive, knowing I'll soon be having a break. We're going to change soon to having four weeks here, four weeks in the nursing home. I think it's the only way I'll be able to keep going.'

Although respite care is one of the most valuable services for carers, setting it up is not without problems. Your relative may feel that you are rejecting her or that respite care is the thin end of the wedge to full-time residential care.

Zahira

'They took Mother into hospital for a week to give us a break. But she wouldn't have it. She cried all the time and didn't eat anything and kept hitting the nurses when they came near her. They were very nice, but after two days they said she'd better come back home.'

Mary

'The first time he was to go to the day centre, he woke me up three times the night before to say, 'I'm not going.' But when they came to fetch him he went as quiet as a lamb. Now he really likes it. He says, 'You get a good dinner, and the women make you laugh.' I think they make a fuss of him because he's the only man. I've arranged for him to go into a home for some respite care for a week in the summer, but I haven't dared to tell him yet. Eventually the plan is that he'll go in one week in six. But we'll take it one step at a time.'

If your relative is very resistant to the idea of respite care, you may find it better to get someone else to talk to her about it. A social worker or doctor or nurse may be able to explain to your relative better than you can why having a break is so important for you.

Ellen

'Setting up the respite care was such a hassle, at the time I wondered if it was really worth it. But now I'm really glad we did it.'

Ask your local social services department about which kinds of respite care are available in your area. Ask about voluntary and private respite arrangements as well as those provided by the local authority.

Living close but not too close

Living close to your relative can cut down on travelling time – and on worry.

Anne

'It used to take us an hour to get there – we had to catch two buses. Then we sold our house and bought one a mile away. We can be there in two minutes now, and if necessary we can walk. It's made all the difference.'

But whether you are living with the person you care for, or caring at a distance, it is important to be able to escape into your own space from time to time.

Marian

'He's taken over the sitting room. He never sits in his room upstairs. It means my husband and I don't often get to be alone together.'

Being well organised

When you're juggling with a lot of different responsibilities, being well organised can help you to survive.

Alison

'We found it quite hard to keep track with so many different people looking after her, so we made out a simple notebook diary for what she'd eaten and what medicine she'd taken, and 'Used the loo?' 'Opened bowels?' with boxes for them to tick.'

Some people seem to be born with a natural organising ability, but for the rest of us these hints may be useful:

- Write a list of things you have to do every day, and tick them off as you go along. If you don't finish the list, carry the items over on to next day's list.
- Keep all the telephone numbers relating to your relative together in one place.
- Keep a diary with dates and times of care arrangements, hospital appointments, meetings with social services, etc.
- Try not to put things off, especially things you don't particularly like doing. Set aside a time each day for making phone calls.
- Plan ahead.

Janet

'When you see your parents getting older, start planning ahead. Don't leave it until a crisis happens.'

Having a supportive family

When you become a carer, there are inevitably extra pressures on your family. It helps a lot to have a partner or children or brothers and sisters who will understand your feelings, share the care with you, and give you emotional support.

Gill

'It's a family effort. My husband and I share the different jobs between us, and our son helps out at weekends or if we're away.'

Kim

'Caring for our parents has brought me closer to my brother and sisters. Last time when I saw my brother, I just burst into tears. He put his arm round me, and said, 'I know how you feel. It's how I felt a month ago."

Getting support from other carers

Many carers find that the friendship and support of other carers is as valuable as the professional help they get. Other carers understand because they have been through the same experiences. They listen without passing judgement or laying blame – they know how difficult it is. Carers also have a wealth of experience and understanding of human emotions – they are good at listening to others. Sometimes, when the person they have been caring for has died, former carers are only too happy to help others in the same position as they have been in. The carers who have contributed their insights and experiences to this book did so because they wanted to help others. Carers are just ordinary people like you.

Susannah

'The first time I went to the carers' meeting I was so nervous I nearly ran away. But as soon as I got in the room, I knew I was in the right place. I opened my mouth to talk, but I found I couldn't say anything – I just cried. Everyone was so nice, and so human. Although they had troubles of their own they took time to listen to me. Now, when a new person comes, I make a point of talking to them.'

You can contact other carers in your area through the Carers National Association or through local Age Concern organisations, local branches of the Alzheimer's Disease Society or other specialist charities (see pp 108–115 for addresses). If there is no carers' group in your area, the Carers National Association can help you to set one up.

Shirley

'I clicked at once with the people I met through the carers' group. I can let my hair down and talk more freely. If it wasn't for the group, I'd be isolated and lonely.'

Hilary

'Once a week I go to the coffee morning at Age Concern. It's the one time of the week when I can really be me.'

Having your own life

It can be hard, when you are caring for someone almost full-time, to find time for yourself. But carers say that having a life of their own is very important to them.

Anne

'The woman from Alzheimer's said, 'Don't give up your job. You won't be a carer for ever, and you need to keep hold of your own life.' It's been hard sometimes, but I'm glad I took her advice.'

Dawn

'What I say to other carers now is, 'Try to keep something for yourself.'
While I was caring for my Mum, I didn't realise how many people I'd just
cut off from. Now that she's died I feel the emptiness. Looking after my
children, keeping my husband happy, caring for my own parents and my
in-laws – I sometimes wondered, 'Where do I fit in?' Now there's only me
and my husband left at home, and I've suddenly got all this time on my
hands. Sometimes I look round and think, 'Well, I'll be blowed. Where
have they all gone?'

Useful addresses

Abbeyfield Society
Housing association specialising in bedsits for older people in shared houses with meals provided.

53 Victoria Street
St Albans
Herts AL1 3UW
Tel: 01727 857536

Accountant of Court
Information about curator bonis in Scotland.

2 Parliament House
Parliament Square
Edinburgh EH1 1RQ
Tel: 0131-225 2595

Action for Dysphasic Adults
Help and information about dysphasia (loss of language).

1 Royal Street
London SE1 7LL
Tel: 0171-261 9572

Alzheimer Scotland – Action on Dementia
Information, support and advice about dementia for people living in Scotland. 24-hour helpline for carers and people with dementia.

22 Drumsheugh Gardens
Edinburgh EH3 7RN
Tel: 0131-225 1453
Helpline: 0800 317 817

Alzheimer's Disease Society
Information, support and advice about caring for someone with Alzheimer's disease.

Gordon House
10 Greencoat Place
London SW1P 1PH
Tel: 0171-306 0606

Arthritis Care
Advice about living with arthritis, loan of equipment, holiday centres. Local branches in many areas.

18 Stephenson Way
London NW1 2HD
Tel: 0171-916 1500

Arthritis and Rheumatism Council
Information about all aspects of
the illness.

Copeman House
St Mary's Court
St Mary's Gate
Chesterfield
Derbyshire S41 7TD
Tel: 01246 558033

Association of Charity Officers
How to find out about charities
which could help you (please write
first).

Beechwood House
Wyllyotts Close
Potters Bar
Herts EN6 2HN
Tel: 01707 651777

Association of Continence Advisers
See Continence Advisory Service

Association of Crossroads Care
Attendant Schemes
See Crossroads Care

BACUP (British Association of
Cancer United Patients)
Support and information for
cancer sufferers and their families.
Freephone advice line for people
outside London.

3 Bath Place
Rivington Street
London EC2A 3JR
Tel: 0171-613 2121 (advice)
0171-696 9003 (admin)
Freephone: 0800 181 199

British Association for Counselling
To find out about counselling services
in your area.

1 Regent Place
Rugby
Warwickshire CV21 2PJ
Tel: 01788 578328/9

British Diabetic Association
Information and advice about living
with diabetes.

10 Queen Anne Street
London W1M 0BD
Tel: 0171-323 1531

British Heart Foundation
Information about all aspects of
heart disease.

14 Fitzhardinge Street
London W1H 4DH
Tel: 0171-935 0185

British Lung Foundation
Information about all aspects of
lung disease.

78 Hatton Garden
London EC1N 8JR
Tel: 0171-831 5831

British Red Cross
Can loan home aids for disabled people. Local branches in many areas.

9 Grosvenor Crescent
London SW1X 7EJ
Tel: 0171-235 5454

Cancer Relief Macmillan Fund
Can put you in touch with the Macmillan nurse service in your area.

Anchor House
15–19 Britten Street
London SW3 3TZ
Tel: 0171-351 7811

CancerLink
Information and advice about all aspects of cancer.

11–21 Northdown Street
London N1 9BN
Tel: 0800 590 415
Asian freephone:
0800 590 415

Care and Repair Ltd
Advice about home repairs and improvements.

Castle House
Kirtley Drive
Nottingham NG7 1LD
Tel: 0115 979 9091

Carers National Association
Information and advice if you are caring for someone. Can put you in touch with other carers and carers' groups in your area.

20–25 Glasshouse Yard
London EC1A 4JS
Tel: 0171-490 8818
(administration)
Carersline:
0171-490 8898
(Mon–Fri 1–4pm)

Centre for Accessible Environments
Information for architects and builders about designing homes for people with disabilities. Has register of architects with experience of this.

60 Gainsford Street
London SE1 2NY
Tel: 0171-357 8182

Chest, Heart and Stroke Association
See Stroke Association, British Heart Foundation *and* British Lung Foundation

Chest, Heart and Stroke Scotland
Confidential advice services by trained nurses.

65 North Castle Street
Edinburgh EH2 3LT
Tel: 0345 720 720
(Mon–Fri
9.30am–12.30pm,
1.30–4pm)

Citizens Advice Bureau
For advice on legal, financial and consumer matters. A good place to turn to if you don't know where to go for help or advice on any subject.

Listed in local telephone directories, or in *Yellow Pages* under 'Social service and welfare organisations'. Other local advice centres may also be listed.

COMBAT
See Huntington's Disease Foundation

Community Health Council
For enquiries or complaints about any aspect of the NHS in your area. Called Health Councils in Scotland.

See the local telephone directory for your area (sometimes listed under Health Authority)

Continence Foundation
Advice and information about whom to contact with incontinence problems.

The Basement
2 Doughty Street
London WC1N 2PH
Tel: 0171-404 6875

Counsel and Care
Advice for older people and their families; can sometimes give grants to help people remain at home, or return to their home.

Lower Ground Floor
Twyman House
16 Bonny Street
London NW1 9PG
Tel: 0171-485 1566

Court of Protection
If you need to take over the financial affairs of someone who is mentally incapable.

Public Trust Office
Protection Division
Stewart House
24 Kingsway
London WC2B 6JX
Tel: 0171-664 7300/7208

Crossroads Care
For a care attendant to come into your home and look after your relative.

10 Regent Place
Rugby
Warwickshire CV21 2PN
Tel: 01788 573653

Dial UK (Disablement Information and Advice Lines)
Information and advice for people with disabilities. Can put you in touch with local contacts.

Park Lodge
St Catherine's Hospital
Tickhill Road
Balby
Doncaster DN4 8QN
Tel: 01302 310123

Disability Law Service
Free legal advice for disabled people and their families.

Room 241
2nd Floor
49–51 Bedford Row
London WC1R 4LR
Tel: 0171-831 8031/7740

Disability Scotland
National organisation for information on all non-medical aspects of disability.

Princes House
5 Shandwick Place
Edinburgh EH2 4RG
Tel: 0131-229 8632
(voice and textphone)

Disabled Living Centres Council
Can tell you your nearest disabled living centre, where you can see and try out aids and equipment.

286 Camden Road
London N7 0BJ
Tel: 0171-700 1707

Disabled Living Foundation
Information about aids to help you cope with a disability.

380–384 Harrow Road
London W9 2HU
Tel: 0171-289 6111

DSS
Formerly the DHSS. The welfare rights and benefits section is called the Benefits Agency.

Freephone 0800 666 555
or see your local telephone directory.

Elderly Accommodation Council
Computerised information about all forms of private and voluntary sector accommodation for older people, by area and/or price range.

46a Chiswick High Road
London W4 1SZ
Tel: 0181-995 8320
Helpline: 0181-742 1182

GRACE
A private agency offering information and help with all aspects of long-term care.

35 Walnut Tree Close
Guildford
Surrey GU1 4UL
Freephone: 0800 137 669

Headway (National Head Injuries Association)
For people who are disabled physically or mentally as a result of a head injury, and their carers,

7 King Edward Court
King Edward Street
Nottingham
NG1 1EW
Tel: 0115 924 0800

Holiday Care Service
Free information and advice about holidays for older or disabled people and their carers.

2nd Floor
Imperial Buildings
Victoria Road
Horley
Surrey RH6 7PZ
Tel: 01293 774535

Incontinence Information Helpline
How to contact your nearest continence adviser.

Tel: 0191-213 0050

Jewish Care
Social care, personal support, residential homes for Jewish people.

Stuart Young House
221 Golders Green Road
London NW11 9DQ
Tel: 0181-485 3282

John Groom's Association for the Disabled
Residential, respite and holiday accommodation.

50 Scrutton Street
London EC2A 4PH
Tel: 0171-452 2000

Local Government Ombudsman
For complaints about your local council which cannot be settled by local officers or councillors

Your nearest Local Government Ombudsman's office will be listed in your local telephone directory.

Mediation UK
Information about local mediation schemes.

82a Gloucester Road
Bristol BS7 8BN
Tel: 0117 924 1234

Network for the Handicapped
See Disability Law Service

New Ways to Work
Advice to individuals and employers about flexible working arrangements.

309 Upper Street
London N1 2TY
Tel: 0171-226 4026

Parkinson's Disease Society
*Information and advice for people
caring for someone with Parkinson's
disease; many local branches.*

22 Upper Woburn Place
London WC1H 0RA
Tel: 0171-383 3513

Pensions Advisory Service
*For queries and problems about
your pension that you cannot sort
out with your employer or pension
provider.*

11 Belgrave Road
London SW1V 1RB
Tel: 0171-233 8080

Public Trust Office
See Court of Protection

**RADAR (Royal Association for
Disability and Rehabilitation)**
*Information about aids and
mobility, holidays, sport and
leisure for disabled people.*

12 City Forum
250 City Road
London EC1V 8AF
Tel: 0171-250 3222

**Relate (formerly National Marriage
Guidance Council)**
*Counselling and help with difficult
relationships; many local branches.*

Herbert Gray College
Little Church Street
Rugby
Warwickshire CV21 3AP
Tel: 01788 573241/
560811

Relatives Association
*Advice for relatives and friends
of people in care homes; works to
improve the quality of care in
care homes.*

5 Tavistock Place
London WC1 9SN
Tel: 0171-916 6055/
0181-201 9153

**Royal Association for Disability
and Rehabilitation**
See RADAR

**Royal National Institute for the
Blind (RNIB)**
*Information and advice for blind
people and their families.*

224 Great Portland Street
London W1N 6AA
Tel: 0171-388 1266

Samaritans
Someone to talk to if you are in despair.

See your local telephone directory.

Standing Conference of Ethnic Minority Senior Citizens
Information, support and advice for older people from ethnic minorities and their families.

5 Westminster Bridge Road
London SE1 7XW
Tel: 0171-928 7861

Stroke Association
Information and advice if you are caring for someone who has had a stroke.

123–127 Whitecross Street
London EC1Y 8JJ
Tel: 0171-490 7999

Trades Union Congress (TUC)
For information about employment rights and trades unions.

Congress House
Great Russell Street
London WC1B 3LS
Tel: 0171-636 0632

United Kingdom Home Care Association (UKHCA)
For information about organisations providing home care in your area.

42 Banstead Road
Carshalton Beeches
Surrey SM5 3NW
Tel: 0181-288 1551

About Age Concern

Choices for the carer of an elderly relative is one of a wide range of publications produced by Age Concern England, the National Council on Ageing. Age Concern cares about all older people and believes later life should be fulfilling and enjoyable. For too many this is impossible. As the leading charitable movement in the UK concerned with ageing and older people, Age Concern finds effective ways to change that situation.

Where possible, we enable older people to solve problems themselves, providing as much or as little support as they need. Our network of 1,400 local groups, supported by 250,000 volunteers, provides community-based services such as lunch clubs, day centres and home visiting.

Nationally, we take a lead role in campaigning, parliamentary work, policy analysis, research, specialist information and advice provision, and publishing. Innovative programmes promote healthier lifestyles and provide older people with opportunities to give the experience of a lifetime back to their communities.

Age Concern is dependent on donations, covenants and legacies.

Age Concern England
1268 London Road
London SW16 4ER
Tel: 0181-679 8000

Age Concern Scotland
113 Rose Street
Edinburgh EH2 3DT
Tel: 0131-220 3345

Age Concern Cymru
4th Floor
1 Cathedral Road
Cardiff CF1 9SD
Tel: 01222 371566

Age Concern Northern Ireland
3 Lower Crescent
Belfast BT7 1NR
Tel: 01232 245729

Other books in this series

The Carer's Handbook: What to do and who to turn to
Marina Lemycka
At some point in their lives millions of people find themselves suddenly responsible for organising the care of an older person with a health crisis. All too often such carers have no idea what services are available or who can be approached for support. This book is designed to act as a first point of reference in just such an emergency, signposting readers on to many more detailed, local sources of advice.
£6.99 0–86242–262–0

Caring for someone who is dying
Penny Mares
Confronting the knowledge that a loved one is going to die soon is always a moment of crisis. And the pain of the news can be compounded by the need to take responsibility for the care and support given in the last months and weeks. This book attempts to help readers cope with their emotions, identify the needs which the situation creates and make the practical arrangements necessary to ensure that the passage through the period is as smooth as possible.
£6.99 0–86242–260–4

Finding and paying for residential and nursing home care
Marina Lewycka
Acknowledging that an older person needs residential care often represents a major crisis for family and friends. Feelings of guilt and betrayal invariably compound the difficulties faced in identifying a suitable care home and sorting out the financial arrangements. This book provides a practical step-by-step guide to the decisions which have to be made and the help which is available.
£6.99 0–86242–261–2

Caring for someone who has dementia
Jane Brotchie
Caring for someone with dementia can be physically and emotionally exhausting, and it is often difficult to think about what can be done to make the situation easier. This book shows how to cope and seek further help as well as containing detailed information on the illness itself and what to expect in the future.
£6.99 0–86242–259–0

Caring for someone who has had a stroke
Philip Coyne and Penny Mares
Although 100,000 people in Britain will have a stroke this year, many people are still confused about what stroke actually means. This book is designed to help carers understand stroke and its immediate aftermath. It contains extensive information on hospital discharge, providing care, rehabilitation, and adjustment to life at home.
£6.99 0–86242–264–7

Caring for Someone with an Alcohol Problem
Mike Ward
When drinking becomes a problem, the consequences for the carer can be physically and emotionally exhausting. This book will help anyone who lives with or cares for a problem drinker, with particular emphasis on caring for an older problem drinker.

£6.99 0-86242-227-2

Caring for Someone at a Distance
Julie Spencer-Cingöz
With people now living longer, sooner or later, we are likely to find ourselves looking after a loved one or a friend – often at a distance. This book will help you to identify the needs and priorities that have to be addressed, offering guidance on the key decisions to be made, minimising risks, what to look for when you visit, how to get the most out of your visits, dealing with your relative's finances and keeping in touch.

£6.99 0-86242-228-0

Publications from Age Concern Books

Money matters

Your Rights: A guide to money benefits for older people
Sally West

A highly acclaimed annual guide to the State benefits available to older people. Contains current information on Income Support, Housing Benefit and Retirement Pensions, among other matters, and provides advice on how to claim.

For further information please telephone 0181-679 8000.

The Pensions Handbook: The pensions system explained
Sue Ward

Many older people in their later working lives become concerned about the adequacy of their existing pension arrangements. This title addresses these worries and suggests strategies by which the value of a prospective pension can be enhanced. Advice is also provided on monitoring company pension schemes.

For further information please telephone 0181-679 8000.

Managing Other People's Money
Penny Letts

Foreword by the Master of the Court of Protection

The management of money and property is usually a personal and private matter. However, there may come a time when someone else has to take over on either a temporary or a permanent basis. This book looks at the circumstances in which such a need could arise and provides a step-by-step guide to the arrangements which have to be made.

£9.99 0-86242-250-7

Housing

A Buyer's Guide to Retirement Housing

Co-published with the National Housing and Town Planning Council

This book answers many of the questions older people may have when looking to buy a flat or bungalow in a sheltered scheme. It provides comprehensive information for older people and their families on topics such as the pros and cons, design and management of schemes, charges and costs, and what to look for.

This popular book – now in its 3rd edition – will provide all the information needed to make an informed decision.

£4.95 0–86242–127–6

Health and care

The Community Care Handbook: The reformed system explained (2nd edition)

Barbara Meredith

The delivery of care in the community has changed dramatically as a result of recent legislation, and continues to evolve. Written by one of the country's foremost experts, this book explains in practical terms the background to the reforms, what they are, how they operate and whom they affect.

£13.99 0–86242–171–3

If you would like to order any of these titles, please write to the address below, enclosing a cheque or money order for the appropriate amount made payable to Age Concern England. Credit card orders may be made on 0181-679 8000.

Mail Order Unit
Age Concern England
1268 London Road
London SW16 4ER

Factsheets from Age Concern

Covering many areas of concern to older people, Age Concern's factsheets are comprehensive and totally up to date. There are over 40 factsheets, with each one providing straightforward information and impartial advice in a simple and easy-to-use format. Topics covered include:

- finding and paying for residential and nursing home care
- raising income from your home
- money benefits
- legal arrangements for managing financial affairs
- finding help at home

Single copies are available free on receipt of a 9" × 12" sae.

Age Concern offers a factsheet subscription service which presents all the factsheets in a folder, together with regular updates throughout the year. The first year's subscription currently costs £40; an annual renewal thereafter is £20.

For further information, or to order factsheets, write to:

Information and Policy Division
Age Concern England
1268 London Road
London SW16 4ER

For readers in Scotland wishing further information, or to order factsheets, please write to:

Age Concern Scotland
113 Rose Street
Edinburgh EH2 3DT

Subscribers in Scotland will automatically be sent Scottish editions of factsheets where law and practice differ in Scotland.

Index